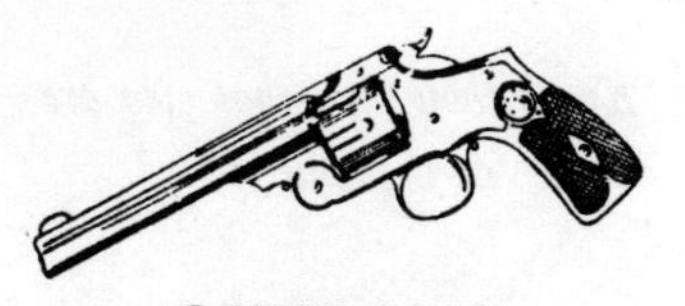

OUTLAWS
OF THE OLD WEST

'Know thou this, that men are
as the time is.'

OUTLAWS
OF THE OLD WEST

*

CARL W. BREIHAN

BONANZA BOOKS
NEW YORK

This edition published by Bonanza Books,
a division of Crown Publishers, Inc.,
by arrangement with the author.
A B C D E F G H

To the Memory of

WALTER HUSTON

an outstanding actor and
an irreplaceable friend

Acknowledgments

I wish to express my sincere appreciation to all those who gave their willing assistance in the task of compiling these facts, many of which are new. I must also make grateful acknowledgment to my friends, Ed Bartholomew and Gregory Gundlach, for their continued encouragement, which has been an inspiration and a great asset. At the same time I humbly thank the various historical societies, newspapers, and collectors, without whose cheerful and invaluable aid I should have had a far more difficult time accomplishing my purpose. To Glenn Clairmonte, I owe much for her willingness to assist whenever it was needed.

C. W. B.

St. Louis, Mo.

Contents

Illustrations

The heading at the beginning of each chapter is a drawing of the gun which was used to kill Jesse James—a Smith and Wesson Model No. 3, .44 calibre, single action, with a 6½-in. barrel

Author's Preface

On a cold, misty night in 1803, two ruffians crept up behind Harry Mason and split his skull wide open with a tomahawk.

The blow ended the career of one of America's most notorious river pirates, for Mason had begun a reckless reign of bloodshed and robbery years before in the Ohio Valley, and was probably the first man to introduce organized crime into America's history.

Living in a large cavern hidden among the bluffs and tangled jungles on the banks of the Ohio River about twenty miles below the mouth of the Wabash, Mason and his gang of cut-throats and highwaymen preyed on pioneers and merchants using the river in their trek west. From Cave-in-the-Rock they could always sweep down on some unsuspecting traveller on the western highway and cut him down.

Mason had moved south as the Ohio Valley became more and more populated. His startling crimes attracted such hearty attention that the governors of Mississippi and Tennessee both offered tremendous dead-or-alive rewards for his capture. He soon became a victim of his own killers, who chopped off his head and carried it up-river to Washington, Mississippi, where they delivered it to lawmen there. It was an unfortunate move on their part, however, since a vigilant lawman recognized one, and they were promptly hanged from the nearest oak-tree.

The Mason gang is a significant ancestor to the outlaw hordes which were to follow in the years of the wild and lawless frontier. Many of Mason's strategic moves were adopted by later gangs and used successfully to loot, plunder, and kill. The gang spawned the first 'squealers' on record. Today the squealer is still an important figure to lawmen. And the gang also graduated two other criminals who were to set out on their own careers of robbery and bloodshed. In later years, outlaw leaders were to be succeeded by lesser members of their gangs. The Mason mob began a grisly heritage which was to be followed in the years to come by such famous and infamous names as Jesse and Frank James, the Youngers, Billy the Kid, the Daltons, the Renos, and Sam Bass—names which were to foster legend and play as glamorous and important a part in the development of America's westward-moving frontier as the railroads or the Army or the just-as-famous lawmen, Wyatt Earp, Bat Masterson, and Pat Garrett. Many times legend has changed the quick-drawing, dead-eyed gunman into an image of the West, and rubbed out the more vicious shadows of his character, leaving behind an exciting and glamorous portrait.

From the Mason gang, however, came two of the most savage, cold-blooded murderers in history, the Harpe Boys, Micajah and Wiley—Big and Little Harpe.

Micajah Big Harpe was a coarse-featured, hulking redhead with a great mat of twisted hair and eyes bright and cold and set apart like those of a snake. His brother was a counterpart, smaller but equally as bestial. They wore tomahawks and knives in their belts and carried rifles. Accompanied by three immoral and vicious mistresses, they moved into Lincoln County, Kentucky, in 1801 to begin a savage crime wave.

It was left to the outraged father of a murdered family to bring the Harpes to justice. The two brutes had secured lodging in the home of a man named Stagall who was on a hunting trip. Posing as ministers, they mistook another lodger for Stagall and murdered him, Mrs. Stagall, and her four children. Then they burned the house to conceal all evidence of the hideous crime.

In the ashes of his home, Stagall found the burned bodies of his family. Each head had been split wide open with a tomahawk—a trademark of Harpe murder.

Enraged to a point of insanity, Stagall and a neighbour, Captain Leeper, tracked the two killers. Near dawn, Stagall and Leeper crept into their camp. One of the women was awakened and screamed an alarm. Little Harpe rolled from his sleeping-bag, plunged into the dark woods, and made good his escape. Big Harpe rushed through the camp, leaped on his horse, and lashed it to a gallop. As he dashed past Leeper, the captain squeezed the trigger of his flintlock and the ball smashed into Harpe's thigh. He crashed howling from the saddle. Stagall pulled up beside him and levelled his gun. The pistol roared and Micajah spun around and fell dead in the road. As a warning to other killers of Harpe ilk, Stagall sliced off the dead thief's head and stuck it on a pole beside the road. The place is known today as Harpe's Head.

A few weeks later Wiley (Little) Harpe was taken in Missouri and hanged. Thus ended the bloody career of the Harpe boys.

There is a vast difference between the outlaws who became famous for their exploits in the mid-eighties and those of the calibre of Mason or the Harpe Boys. Truth and legend have become almost synonymous when referring to the James brothers or the Youngers or Doolin or Rube Burrow or Sam Bass.

In the glory days of the American West, when the nation was still learning to walk, men like the Youngers and the James brothers brought fame and a certain necessary pride to parts of the country which otherwise might never have gained any greater distinction than being a name on a map.

St. Joseph, Missouri, first gained notoriety as the place where Jesse James was slain. Billy the Kid brought fame to Fort Sumner and many other towns in New Mexico. And Tombstone became a household word because of its fiery history as a city of fast-shooting, fast-dying gunmen.

The same might also be said for Jackson County, Missouri, which produced the Younger brothers. Their story, more than any other, probably shows to what extremes emotions were aroused towards the West's bandits. Cole, Jim, and Bob Younger began their careers as heroes of the Confederacy and ended them in dismal solitude behind prison walls. But even during their years in Minnesota's Stillwater Prison they spawned a legal battle that lasted nearly twenty-six years and stirred the imagination of two entire States—one with complete admiration, the other with hatred.

Today the fading records of St. Clair and Jackson Counties still recount the true story of the Youngers—documentary on the extent to which emotions ran during the heyday of the outlaw and gunman.

The lives of bandits and outlaws often caused emotions to burn deep. In Austin, after King Fisher was shot to death in the Variety Theatre massacre, newspapermen wrote of the great 'tragedy' and damned the Press and lawmen of San Antonio for 'covering up facts' in the death. Yet Fisher and his companion victim in the fatal shooting, Ben Thompson, were both notorious outlaws and gunmen—hardly the types to be championed by the Press even in death.

Sam Bass, whose trail of gunfire and robbery covered half a dozen States and lasted for three years, was the subject of several sympathetic, almost poetic, pieces following his death at Round Rock.

Jesse and Frank James were loved and respected by as many newspaper people and citizens as hated them. Their exploits fostered many arguments and even caused families to split in disagreement.

It is at this point that truth and legend have sometimes become so interwoven that it is difficult to separate them; but I have tried to cover each character in an authentic manner. I have taken the necessary time and trouble to verify reports, and have exhausted every possibility to include all that is known.

For many years I have been making a study of the American outlaw, and this book is an honest endeavour to describe an era of crime without bugle-blowing or banner-waving. I have especially tried not to show any personal bias; I know full well that it is easy for a writer to become so engrossed in his material that his better judgment becomes warped or slanted. Many who have commented on the famous outlaws have made martyrs of their subjects, but they have forgotten or neglected those who were truly martyrs to law and order. Others have treated serious matters with levity or with disbelief, and surely that is their privilege. But also, when those who claim to favour law and order take an apologetic stand regarding outrages perpetrated by the forces of the law, they should be reminded that a law-enforcement officer has no more right to do wrong than the criminal has to commit a crime.

Many stories told of the various American outlaws and badmen are true, others are refined fables—truth seeded from legend, or a mixture of both. The saga of the West is a story in which a lawman and an outlaw were often distinguished only by a badge. It is the story of a time in history when quick death hung on an angry oath or sometimes even a simple bet. The West provided the most notable arena in America's colourful history. Many tales have been written about that arena—as it was born, as it grew, and as it matured—at gunpoint.

1959 C. W. B.

I *The James and Younger Boys*

THE most popular outlaw in the history of the West is Jesse James, the Missouri highway robber and bank bandit whose daring exploits still stir the imagination.

Everyone who knew him personally has reported that he inherited Southern charm and courtesy from his Kentucky parents. His father was the Reverend Robert James of Georgetown, Kentucky, who married the young orphan Zerelda Cole and took her with him to Missouri. There in Clay County their two famous sons, Frank and Jesse, were born in 1844 and 1847 respectively, and there also their third child, Susan, arrived in 1849.

With such a family as incentive it is not surprising that Mr. James decided to seek a fortune and let himself be rushed with the populace to the California goldfields. But within a few days of his arrival there he died, in August 1851. Zerelda did her best to rear her children, but frontier conditions made the task very difficult indeed. A neighbouring farmer, Benjamin Simms, offered to make life easier for her, and she married him. Simms died shortly afterwards; at least, before long Zerelda was again calling herself Mrs. James. When Jesse was ten years old she gave him a new father, another native of Kentucky—Dr. Reuben Samuel, who for the rest of his life showed a truly paternal interest in Frank and Jesse and Susan.

In the backwoods country of Missouri Zerelda raised her

children strictly, never forgetting that their father had been a minister of the Gospel. She was known to idolize Frank ('Mister Frank', as she always called him), but it is certain that she dearly loved Jesse and Susan also. There has long been a rumour that Jesse was a love child, and although this has never been substantiated, it is true that Jesse was sensitive on the subject. It has even been said that part of his drive to domineer his older brother in their later gang career stemmed from his suspicion that there might be something in his own history which he had to overcome. In that wild land, where a gunbelt was part of the proper equipment of every able-bodied man, these boys both assumed manhood long before their time and became crack shots as a matter of course.

During the 1850's, in every Missouri community there were violent quarrels on the subject of slavery and even secession. The James boys were exposed to the constant disputes and learned not to be surprised when neighbours were injured or even buried after a forthright Missouri-Kansas border discussion. To them it became as natural as daylight that men should decide what was right by the use of pistol or rifle.

The James boys were governed by Southern sympathies because of their family background, but they had a tangible reason to become partisans against slavery haters. The wandering bands of armed men called Jayhawkers, or Red Legs, aroused the indignation of every self-respecting citizen. These marauders, led by James H. Lane or James Montgomery or Charles Jennison, left so much death and destruction in their wake that in the 1860's the pro-Confederate faction tried to check them by forming bands of their own. The most notorious of these bands was the one led by William Clarke Quantrill, who, with personal reasons for hating Kansans and a personal pleasure in a good fight, had come to Missouri and announced his determination to defend the border from the Jayhawkers.

In the early part of the Civil War Frank James enlisted on the side of the South. In the battle of Wilson's Creek he was captured and given field parole—that is, on giving his word that he would not take up arms again he was allowed to go home. However, he was a young braggart at the time, and boasted that he wasn't afraid of any Northern soldiers. A conscientious sheriff arrested him, and it took a little while for his mother to use her influence among friends and effect his release from jail. By then he was distinctly disgruntled—'All right, if that's the way they want it!'—and he gave himself the luxury of taking back his promise not to fight any more. He rode off to join Quantrill's gang.

It was this impetuous move of Frank's which started the unfortunate chain of events for the James family—for, as soon as it was known that Frank had joined Quantrill, the Militia began to harass his family. In 1863 a company of bluecoats appeared at Dr. Samuel's home. They found young Jesse and his stepfather ploughing and demanded the whereabouts of Quantrill's men. The officer in charge did not believe them when they said they had no idea where the guerrillas were hiding out.

Some of the soldiers jabbed their bayonets into Jesse's legs to stimulate his memory. They also whipped him with ropes, but he gritted his teeth and looked at them with glowing hatred. Dr. Samuel attempted to prevent the soldiers from torturing the boy, and in anger the officer commanded his men to throw a rope around the doctor's neck and hoist him up a tree. They gave him several jerks in an effort to induce him to answer their questions. After they had ridden away, Zerelda was able to revive her husband—though the rope burns on his neck were a permanent souvenir of the occasion.

Jesse was nearly sixteen years old and had long been in a hurry to grow up and use his gun against the Jayhawkers. Now that the State Militiamen had humiliated him and his stepfather, he felt he could wait no longer, and made preparations to run away and find his brother Frank. As though they suspected this, the Militiamen returned and carried Jesse off to the jail in Liberty, Missouri. Perhaps their main purpose was to frighten him, for they soon sent him back home. But the next move they made was to carry his mother and little sister Susan off to the St. Joseph jail. When he learned that Susan had contracted a fever in the filthy jail and almost died, he had to find an outlet in action.

He sought Quantrill and begged to be allowed to ride with his brother and the other guerrillas. Quantrill wanted to reject him because he was such a pale and slender youth, but Bloody Bill Anderson liked his spunk and offered to look out for the lad if Quantrill would take him on. Jesse was overjoyed when he was allowed to participate in an attack on the Federal garrison at Richfield on May 19, 1863. He had his first taste of victory when Captain Sessions, the garrison commander, was killed and the soldiers under him suffered an ignominious defeat.

Jesse stopped by to see his mother in the middle of the night, and she told him that Plattsburg was being left virtually undefended. So he slipped back to the Quantrill camp and gave his news. He rode between his brother and the daring Quantrill as they attacked Plattsburg and captured a large supply of ammunition and money. After that he was no longer called 'the Dingus', but was accepted as a full-fledged guerrilla. In September 1861 the Jayhawkers had wantonly sacked the town of Osceola, Missouri, and in vengeful retaliation Quantrill led his men to lay waste the town of Lawrence, Kansas. According to Captain Harrison Trow and Cole Younger, on that occasion young Jesse was not one of the men selected to ride, so he sulked in camp, waiting for his brother Frank to return and tell him all about it.

On September 23, 1864, more than fifty of his fellow guerrillas were camped near the Howard-Boone County line, when their scout returned to report that about ninety Federal Militiamen were coming along the road to Rocheport. Instantly the guerrillas mounted, rode to the main road, and formed ranks eight abreast across the route of the Federal company. When the Union soldiers approached, Quantrill's men gave a piercing Rebel yell, and they broke ranks in disorder, surrendering their supply train. Thirty were killed before darkness fell and enabled the rest to retreat.

The following day the guerrillas were still rejoicing over this success when they set out to join Confederate General Price's company. During the march they encountered some fighting at Fayette, and on September 27 reached a spot south-east of Centralia, Missouri. Here they stopped a stage-coach from Columbia and searched the passengers to be sure they were not Federal sympathizers.

Just as they were allowing the coach to resume its journey, they saw a westbound passenger train pulling up. Bloody Bill Anderson insisted on dragging twenty-three Union soldiers out of the cars. One of them Anderson selected to hold as hostage for a pal of his who had been captured, but the remaining twenty-two (on leave, headed for their homes) he killed in cold blood. The train was then set on fire, the throttle in the engine opened, and it rolled wildly down the track. Jesse was too thrilled over this exploit to come to any decision as to whether he liked it or not, but it taught him a certain technique of brutality.

Anderson picked Jesse as one of ten to watch Major Johnson's troops, who were trying to catch the guerrillas. Riding at a safe distance from Johnson's lines, they started shooting, rode off a way, then stopped to shoot again. Just as they had hoped, Major Johnson set out to chase them, waving a Navy dragoon revolver. Thus he walked into the trap, and sixty of his men were instantly killed, while the others fled. Jesse himself had shot the Major. He took the belt and revolver from the body as souvenirs.

Within a few days the guerrillas themselves were ambushed. Jesse's horse was shot from under him, and he was wounded in the left side and arm. This was the first time he had been wounded. He expected to die and sent a message to his mother. But he was soon feeling better, if not immediately able to ride and fight.

While camped four miles from Independence, he wanted to be useful in some way, so he dressed up as a girl—his handsome, clear-cut face and slender form made this possible—and slipped into town to see what he could learn about the enemy. He went calling on the madam of a house where the gay girls laughed at his disguise, and they told him proudly how popular they were with the Federal officers. That night Quantrill's men hid in the brush nearby, and they killed a dozen bluecoats who had meant to call on the hospitable girls.

At Flat Rock Ford, near the Grand River, on August 13, 1864, Jesse James nearly met his death. About sixty-five encamped guerrillas were surprised by three hundred Federal soldiers and about one hundred and fifty Red Legs. Jesse was struck in the lung by a musket ball and lay neglected when his side retreated. After dark he crawled to shelter, and a family named Rudd nursed him back to health.

When the Confederate forces under Generals Price and Shelby withdrew from Missouri for tactical reasons many of the guerrillas managed to take a change of scene, and Jesse himself rode to Texas with Lieutenant George Shepherd. As they were on their way through the Cherokee Nation—now Oklahoma—to their surprise they came face to face with Captain Emmett Goss's company of Federal Militiamen. Jesse singled out the leader and sent bullets through his brain and heart. When Goss fell his men scattered.

In the spring of 1865 General Robert E. Lee surrendered to General Ulysses S. Grant at Appomattox. Jesse James was by this time a hardened and experienced guerrilla fighter. He was carrying a flag of truce as he rode at the head of a group of guerrillas on their way to surrender to Major Rogers at Lexington, Missouri. A Federal trooper, evidently not recognizing the flag of truce, shot Jesse through the same lung that had been wounded before. Because his companions believed that he was dead his name was not listed as one of those surrendering.

He was wearing a flannel shirt at the time. The bullet

carried a piece of this cloth into the wound, and perhaps it helped to stop the flow of blood. Months later he coughed up small recognizable bits of the flannel. By good fortune he was found in time to be nursed back to health. As soon as he could travel again, he joined his mother in Rulla, Nebraska, where she had been banished because of her outspoken Confederate sympathies. She had her son moved to Kansas City, where he was lovingly nursed by his young cousin, Zerelda Mimms. Nobody knew then that he would later marry her and that she would devote herself to him until his death.

Since Jesse had not been listed as surrendering, he was considered an outlaw, and constantly harried by Federal partisans and troops. One bitter night, February 18, 1867, Jesse was at the Samuel homestead in Kearney when six Militiamen rode up. Jesse was still suffering from the wound in his lung, but he fought them off with a pair of revolvers, and it is said killed several. Before another contingent could arrive he started for California to visit his uncle, Woodson James, who owned the Paso Robles Hot Sulphur Springs in San Luis, Obsipo County. Frank was there also, recovering from his own wounds.

The next that was heard of the James brothers was a year later, after a bank robbery, when a horse one of the robbers had been riding was identified as Jesse's. A warrant was issued for him, and the sheriff went to the Samuels' home—but his horse was shot from under him as he approached. Then Jesse fled again, this time to Tennessee. At least, it is said that about this time he arrived at the Tennessee home of a widow of one of Quantrill's men. When she told him that within an hour she expected the local banker to arrive with the sheriff, to dispossess her because she could not pay a five-hundred-dollar mortgage, Jesse gave her the money and went into the woods. After she had redeemed the mortgage he waylaid the banker and relieved him of the five hundred dollars.

Jesse stopped to call at General Shelby's home in time to see a Negro boy attacked by a white mob bent on lynching him.

Jesse stepped up and offered to kill any man who touched the boy, and the mob dispersed—but only after recognizing him. This made it necessary for him to keep moving.

Jesse had been shaken with righteous indignation when the Missouri State Constitution was adopted on April 8, 1865. It stipulated that no former Confederate soldiers or sympathizers should be permitted to practise any profession, though it granted amnesty to all who had been Union soldiers. This meant that Jesse and his friends had to lead wary lives. Once he found four of his former companions hanging from the branch of a tree. Because they had not been yanked from their saddles, but had been lifted from the ground, their necks had not been broken. They were revived. Such incidents did not salve the hot tempers, but rather encouraged the life of outlawry, and the series of bank robberies which followed may be seen as the outcome of official violence.

On February 13, 1866, a daring band robbed the Commercial Bank at Liberty of nearly seventy-five thousand dollars. Since Jesse was at the time suffering from his lung wound and unable to ride, it is not likely that he was one of the robbers, but he was actually accused of instigating it.

When the old Southern Bank of Kentucky at Russellville was robbed Jesse was accused by Nimrod Long, the president of the bank. Mr. Long had years before paid the bills of a certain Baptist minister at Georgetown, Kentucky—Robert James!—and he felt it unfair that Jesse, the son, should commit an unfriendly act. He said that, among the eight men involved in that robbery, it was Jesse who scuffled with him in the hall and shot him twice, grazing his head. In this instance the outlaws tied up the cashier, Morton Barkley, and scooped up fourteen thousand dollars—failing to find the fifty thousand in the vault.

Not long before Christmas in 1869 the bank of Gallatin, Missouri, was raided by a band of armed men who intimidated the citizenry by Wild West shooting into the air. Captain John Sheets, the bank's cashier, was shot. Since Sheets had been an officer in the Missouri Federal Militia, there was strong suspicion that Jesse and Frank James had been the murderers. On hearing this, those young men boldly rode into Kearney and strongly denied the accusation. They wrote to the Governor of Missouri, and the governor made a public statement to the effect that he did not believe they were guilty.

On April 27, 1872, five strangers rode up to the Deposit Bank of Columbia in the south-central part of Kentucky, in Adair County. Three of them dismounted and entered the bank. The other two took positions from where they could command the street, drew heavy Colt revolvers, and with a hearty Rebel yell began shooting and telling everyone to get into the houses. Inside the bank three executives were seated at a table when the robber who seemed to be Jesse James said gruffly: 'This is a holdup. If you don't wanna get your damned head shot off, don't start nothing. We mean business. No damned fool tricks out o'you, or I'll drill you.'

When Judge Barnett cried out for help he was struck with the barrel of a revolver, and his hand was shot.

One robber was shoving a heavy revolver into the face of Mr. Martin, the cashier, and saying. 'Open up that safe. Be quick about it, or I'll spatter your damn brains all over Adair County.'

Mr. Martin reached to a desk drawer for a revolver and a 45-calibre slug tore through his head.

After looting the bank of all the money in sight—about fifteen hundred dollars—the three bandits joined their lookouts and fled south. Although a posse followed and a reward was offered for their capture, they never were caught.

On May 27, 1873, another bank job supposedly masterminded by Jesse James occurred at the St. Genevieve (Missouri) Savings Association. It was early in the morning, and the cashier, O. D. Harris, had just entered the bank. The bandits fled with about four thousand dollars before the citizenry discovered they had taken the cashier along as a shield or hostage. Harris was released, but again nothing came of the search.

On June 28, 1871, there was a robbery as far away as

Corydon, Iowa. The heavily armed robbers ordered the cashier and book-keeper and customers to stay quiet or die. The safe was opened for them, they scooped up the money, and left before any outcry could be raised.

The first train robbery credited to Jesse James and his gang took place on July 21, 1873, at three o'clock in the morning, a mile and a half from the whistle-stop at Adair, Iowa. The robbers had pried loose a rail on a curve of the Chicago, Rock Island, and Pacific track. When the train hit the loose rail the locomotive toppled over, the engineer was killed, and the fireman injured. The outlaws rifled the express car, then sauntered through the train relieving passengers of money, jewellery, and other valuables. The inevitable posse organized by the sheriff trailed the band as far as St. Clair County, Missouri, before abandoning the chase.

The next hint of the whereabouts of the James brothers came in September, when two horsemen thundered up to the gates of the Kansas City Fair and took possession, at gun point, of about ten thousand dollars in gate receipts before they rode blithely away.

And even stage robberies were not beneath the dignity of the mysterious bandits, as was proved by their attack on the Arkansas coach service between Malvern and the fashionable Hot Springs in January 1874. This time they made a haul of nearly three thousand five hundred dollars.

A second train robbery occurred at Gads Hill, on the line between St. Louis and Little Rock, Arkansas. At three-thirty in the afternoon of January 31, 1874, seven men took over the station, placing the stationmaster under guard. They set the semaphore signal at STOP to be sure the southbound train from St. Louis would pull up. It did, at six that evening, and the robbers looted the safe in the express car and rifled the pockets of the passengers. The train proceeded to Piedmont, Missouri, the nearest station with telegraph apparatus, and news of the holdup was sent to Little Rock and St. Louis.

The posse followed clues as far as Stanton, Missouri, and for more than a week camped patiently at the entrance of a cave where they believed the robbers had hidden. When they finally thought it was safe to investigate they found the robbers' horses inside, but not the men. It was later learned that the outlaws had been able to swim out of the cave by means of an underground river.

In 1874 the Pinkerton Detective Agency was engaged by the railroads and banks to put a stop to these depredations. They sent their shrewdest operator, J. W. Whicher, to Liberty to apprehend the James brothers. On the road between Independence and Blue Mills, Whicher was found shot through the head and the heart. Allan Pinkerton was convinced that Frank and Jesse James had committed this murder, and he laid careful plans to punish them. On the night of January 25, 1874, his detectives surrounded the Samuel home and tossed through the window a thirty-two-pound iron bomb wrapped in flaming kerosene-saturated rags. The bomb exploded and a piece tore off Mrs. Samuel's right arm below the elbow and killed her little son Archie. The James brothers were upstairs at the time. They climbed out the window and slid down the roof to get away. There was a skirmish in the dark, but they managed to get their horses out of the barn and escape. In the face of their steady fire the detectives ran into the woods.

After this atrocity sentiment in favour of the James family was so strong that in March 1875 General Jeff Jones of Callaway County introduced into the Missouri House of Representatives a Bill offering amnesty to Frank and Jesse for crimes during the war of which they had been accused if, in return, they would agree to stand trial for crimes charged against them since the close of the war.

Perhaps the reason the Bill was defeated was that about this time a neighbour of the Jameses, Daniel H. Askew, who had helped the Pinkerton agents, was shot while returning to his house with a bucket of water from the spring. It was determined that his murderer had been hiding behind a pile of wood. The James boys were suspected, though friends of the family claimed that some enemy had killed Askew in order to throw doubt upon them and defeat the amnesty Bill.

There is no question that Jesse was blamed for many crimes he did not commit. Sometimes two robberies were perpetrated at the same time, hundreds of miles apart, and at both scenes people swore they saw Jesse.

At seven o'clock on April 7, 1874, the regular mail stage between Austin and San Antonio, Texas, was stopped thirty miles south-west of Austin. Among the passengers was C. Breckenridge, president of the First National Bank of San Antonio, who was carrying a thousand dollars in his pocket. The robbers cut loose all but one of the horses, and the stage reached its destination several hours late. It never has been proved whether this was one of Jesse's jobs or not.

Jesse was by this time married to his cousin Zee, and they had three children, a son and twin boys who died in infancy while they were hiding out in Nashville, Tennessee, under an assumed name. Later they had a daughter, Mary.

Aside from his devotion to Zee and their children, Jesse had a strong family loyalty. For instance, he had always cherished his sister Susan. When she planned to marry Allen Parmer, whom he hated, he tried to commit suicide. Only an all-night vigil by his family enabled him to throw off the effects of the sixteen grains of morphine he had taken.

It is amazing how much time he was able to spend with his loved ones in spite of the constant watch the law-enforcement officers set upon everyone he knew.

It was generally believed that Jesse's gang looted the bank at Huntington, West Virginia, on September 1, 1875. On that day four well-mounted men, wearing long linen dust-coats, rode up to the bank. Two dismounted and entered, leaving the others outside. Cashier Robert T. Oney didn't argue, but opened the safe when ordered to do so, and the robbers were gone within a few minutes.

This time the sheriff's party chased them diligently and sent a description of the men to all the newspapers. There was even a skirmish in the woods near Pine Hill, in Rockcastle County, and, though three of the robbers escaped, Tom McDaniels was wounded and was carried to the Dillons' farmhouse. After he died three strangers stopped at the house and asked to see the corpse.

On December 13, 1875, the little railroad station of Muncie, near Kansas City, was held up by a band of armed men in the same manner in which the Gads Hill holdup had been effected. The semaphore signal at STOP halted the train, and two of the robbers kept their guns trained on the engine crew, while the others entered the express car and forced the messenger to open the safe. They took away from thirty to fifty thousand dollars in gold, and this remained another unsolved crime on the police blotter.

A train was held up at Rocky Cut, near Otterville, Missouri, on the night of July 8, 1876. This time the robbers did not set a STOP signal, but waved a red lantern to halt the train. They did not molest the passengers—merely took seventeen thousand dollars from the express-car safe. A local man named Hobbs Kerry was arrested on suspicion when found digging a hole in his garden to hide a thousand dollars, and in his confession said Frank and Jesse James had been in the party. Angrily Jesse wrote a denial to the editor of the *Kansas City Times*, mailing his letter at Oak Grove, Kansas, under date of August 14.

The robbery which did more than anything else to cripple the James gang was the raid on the First National Bank at Northfield, Minnesota, on the morning of September 7, 1876. This bank was located in the south end of the two-storey building called the Scriver Block, on the corner of Division Street and Bridge Square, near an alley behind two hardware stores. Across the street from the Scriver Block was the Dampier House, where the town physician, Dr. H. M. Wheeler, happened to be.

In this case it is definitely known that Jesse and Frank James were in the party, and their companions were the three Younger brothers (Cole, Jim, and Bob), Clell Miller (otherwise known as William Stiles), and Charlie Pitts (sometimes travelling under the name of Sam Wells). The plan, which Jesse had outlined before the gang left camp, was for Bob Younger and Charlie Pitts to wait for the rest of them in the square. Bob Younger, ordinarily a temperate young bandit, had been nipping the bottle and was a bit fuzzy in his reactions. Frank James too had apparently been drinking. Although Frank was usually able to handle liquor well, he was inclined to be trigger-happy when he had taken a few.

The first group, posing as loafers, became impatient to start the job. As their friends rode into view they walked into the bank. When Cole Younger and Clell Miller saw that they had already started, they hurried to the bank building, where the door had been left open.

Cole said to Miller, 'Shut the door quick!' and he dismounted, leaning over as though he had to tighten the saddle girth.

J. S. Allen, standing in the doorway of his hardware store, went over to the bank to see what was happening. Miller levelled a gun at him and cried out, 'Get away from here!'

Allen turned around at once and edged around the corner of the building, but as soon as he was out of sight he shouted: 'Get your guns, boys! They're robbing the bank!'

Cole Younger fired a shot into the air to signal the rear-guard bandits at the bridge that the plan was not going as well as expected. Almost immediately he heard a shot from inside the bank—and the three outlaws in the rear began shooting to clear pedestrians off the streets. One man who came innocently walking towards them was a Swedish immigrant who could not understand English. When he continued walking he was shot dead. There has been a long argument as to whether one of the outlaws fired that shot or he was the victim of a stray bullet from the embattled citizens.

To the inhabitants of Northfield the call for defence against armed bandits revived memory of Indian warfare. They grabbed their shotguns and ran into the square. Miller was just mounting his horse when Elias Stacy peppered his face with

REWARD!

- DEAD OR ALIVE -

$5,000.00 will be paid for the capture of the men who robbed the bank at

NORTHFIELD, MINN.

They are believed to be Jesse James and his Band, or the Youngers.

All officers are warned to use precaution in making arrest. These are the most desperate men in America.

Take no chances! Shoot to kill!!

J. H. McDonald,

SHERIFF

A poster issued after the famous Northfield Bank robbery

birdshot. Another citizen, A. R. Manning, came out with a breech-loading rifle and fired at Charlie Pitts. His horse fell dead, so Charlie leaped up behind Miller.

Cole Younger yelled to his friends inside the bank: 'Come on! It's time for a getaway!' but just then Mr. Manning fired his breech-loader again and wounded him in the thigh.

About eighty yards away Bill Chadwell was holding his excited horse, ready to start off the instant the others were out of the bank, but a bullet from Manning's breech-loader hit him in the heart.

In the meantime, Dr. Wheeler fired his rifle from a second-storey window of the Dampier House, but his aim was too high to hit Jim Younger. Jim looked around angrily, to locate the sharpshooter, but instead saw Clell Miller get his death bullet from Dr. Wheeler's second try. Just then Bob Younger came running out of the bank, and Dr. Wheeler fired, wounding him in the right elbow. Bob made the border shift, landing his pistol in his left hand, but he had an awkward time untying the horses with a left hand holding a gun.

In the confusion the bandits left without collecting any money, but they had shot the bank's book-keeper, Joseph Lee Heywood, in the head, and he was dying as they fled. Leaving Miller's body where it had fallen, they galloped out of Northfield along the Dundas road. Near Mankato they separated as previously planned, and Frank and Jesse James rode rapidly west.

Governor John S. Pillsbury of Minnesota offered a large reward for the capture of any of the surviving bandits. On September 21 a farm boy reported seeing suspicious characters in the neighbourhood of Madelia. A quickly formed posse surrounded the Youngers and Charlie Pitts, hungry in their swamp hideout. Six men volunteered to rout them out. In the violent fight Charlie Pitts was killed, Jim Younger got five bullets, one shattering his upper jaw, Cole got eleven, and Bob was shot through the right lung. The three Youngers were herded together and taken to Madelia.

Few people realize that the Younger brothers came from a a highly respected and influential family in Lee's Summit. Their grandfather, Charles Younger, was an early settler and landowner. His will is still among the yellow documents in the county courthouse. Harry Younger, father of the famous trio, was a United States mail contractor for many years before he was shot down in cold blood and robbed.

At that time, Coleman Younger was a college student with an honourable record of service during the War between the States. Returning home from college when his father was killed, Cole Younger made a vow of revenge.

'I then and there vowed eternal vengeance for this crime against my father,' he said later, 'and I carried it out, but in so doing I've glutted myself with other men's blood, ruined the family honour, and damned my own soul.'

Ironically, this vow made by Cole Younger against the villains who had killed his father resulted in his own career of crime, a career which ended with the Northfield bank robbery and the capture of Cole, Jim, and Bob, in the swamp near Madelia. Here history leaves the Youngers. Many believe the Youngers died at Madelia, others that Cole was killed and the other two brothers escaped. Actually all three were critically wounded, but survived. Jim was shot in the face by Captain T. L. Vought, who was standing only ten feet away. The bullet split his upper lip; blew away half his jaw and penetrated the back part of his throat, lodging in the muscles. Two years later the bullet was removed by a hospital steward named Clark at Stillwater Prison.

After the capture of the Youngers, however, there began one of the bitterest court fights in legal history. For twenty-five years the Honourable W. C. Bronaugh, Company K, 16th Missouri Infantry, C.S.A., battled for the release of the Youngers. Sympathy was keen in many quarters. People felt that the Youngers had been driven to their lives of crime and banditry. But the memory of the Northfield bank robbery was still vivid in the minds of many citizens in Minnesota. Their attitude towards most citizens of Missouri became one of resentment.

The Youngers were captured and sentenced in 1876, but it was not until 1882 that Bronaugh managed to secure a letter of introduction to Warden A. J. Reed at the State Prison. Reed received him with cold reserve, but Bronaugh was permitted to see Cole, Bob, and Jim, and it is hard to imagine his feelings as he stood before these three men who had fought so valiantly under him for the Confederacy and who now were as helpless as infants. Bronaugh outlined his plans to obtain their paroles and left. During the next three years he worked tirelessly for their release. He managed a meeting with Governor William R. Marshall of Minnesota, and things began to appear favourable. People in Missouri rejoiced. In Minnesota Governor Marshall was assailed when his intention to assist the three men to get a pardon became known. He made a speech on behalf of the notorious brothers, but public opinion prevented him from signing the pardon papers.

Three more years went by. Major Edwards, a friend of the Youngers, drew up a petition and presented it to William Merriam, then Governor of Minnesota. At the same time Bronaugh circulated a petition for their release through the Missouri Legislature. Twenty-eight senators and every member of the House of Representatives signed the petition. B. G. Yates, the man who had shot one of the Youngers at Madelia, and Captain W. W. Murphy, another prominent actor in the dramatic capture, both joined the cause in favour of the Youngers and wrote letters to the governor requesting their release. Many requests in their favour came from Faribault, the town in which they were tried and sentenced.

But Governor Merriam refused to grant the pardon. Feeling against the Youngers was still high in Northfield, especially among the friends of Heywood, the dead bookkeeper. Merriam's refusal was the deathblow to Bob Younger, who had been suffering from consumption for several years. He died on September 16, 1889, inside the bleak prison walls which had been his dismal home for thirteen years.

Seven more years crawled by, and Bronaugh continued

PROCLAMATION

\$5,000.00

REWARD

FOR EACH of SEVEN ROBBERS of THE TRAIN at WINSTON, MO., JULY 15, 1881, and THE MURDER of CONDUCTER WESTFALL

\$ 5,000.00

ADDITIONAL for ARREST or CAPTURE

DEAD OR ALIVE

OF JESSE OR FRANK JAMES

THIS NOTICE TAKES the PLACE of ALL PREVIOUS REWARD NOTICES.

CONTACT SHERIFF, DAVIESS COUNTY, MISSOURI IMMEDIATELY

T. T. CRITTENDEN, GOVERNOR
STATE OF MISSOURI
JULY 26, 1881

One of the public proclamations which made life difficult for Jesse and Frank James doggedly to battle on behalf of the two remaining Youngers. Governor Clough, the new chief executive of Minnesota, was beseeched by the Youngers' champion for their pardons. He turned the entire matter over to the newly organized Pardon and Parole Board of Minnesota. Such men as T. T. Crittenden and the Honourable Champ Clark submitted testimonials on their behalf. The pardon was still refused.

Finally, on July 10, 1901, the Minnesota State Legislature passed a Bill favouring the pardon. Bronaugh's battle was won. On July 14, 1901, Cole and Jim Younger stepped outside the prison walls for the first time in twenty-five years.

But even then their lives were marked with tragedy. Minnesota justice followed Jim Younger to his grave. Unable to leave Minnesota because of a clause in their pardon, the two men found it hard to get work. Jim's sweetheart was unable to marry him because the Board refused them permission to wed. They tried their hands at insurance writing, but learned that any insurance policy written by them would not be honoured by insurance companies. Destitute and demoralized, Jim Younger shot himself to death one Sunday afternoon in October 1902, in the Reardon Hotel at St. Paul. Tender hands carried his body back to Lee's Summit, Missouri, where he was laid to rest next to Bob and the other members of the Younger family.

A year later the Board of Pardons finally granted Cole Younger permission to return to his beloved Missouri. He returned to Lee's Summit, welcomed by friends. There he opened a business and lived happily until March 21, 1916.

The Northfield bank episode was the saddest in the career of the James gang. It not only reduced their numbers, but generally made them so unpopular that thereafter it was impossible to recruit new members. However, it did not keep the James brothers from perpetrating a number of other robberies, even without a full complement of helpers.

The authorities were desperately in need of some means to stop them before the public lost all faith in the law. Sheriff

Timberlake finally worked out a little plot, with the approval of Governor T. T. Crittenden of Missouri—the same man who later, when Consul-General of the United States, signed a testimonial on behalf of the imprisoned Younger brothers. He engaged Charley and Bob Ford to try for the reward offered on Jesse's head.

The Fords had rather unsavoury reputations, and Sheriff Timberlake knew they were in no position to refuse to co-operate, since he was offering them pardon for previous crimes. Jesse had recently been trying to enlist their services, and he invited them to visit him so that they could discuss strategy. They put on an innocent act as his guests. They knew he was too quick on the draw to let them shoot him if he ever caught on to their intentions, and he was always wearing his gunbelt.

On the morning of April 3, 1882, Jesse and the Fords finished eating breakfast in the kitchen with Zee and the two children. Jesse walked into the living-room with Charley and Bob, and in a relaxed gesture flung his gunbelt to the bed on which he had spent the night. Then he climbed on a chair with a feather duster and brushed some dust off the frame of a picture.

Charley Ford winked at his brother, and Bob drew his gun. When the trigger was cocked the sound alerted Jesse, and he turned. But the bullet was already on its way. He fell headlong off the chair, dead before he hit the floor.

Jesse's wife ran from the kitchen with the children, and in her grief she knelt beside her beloved's body as Bob Ford put his gun back into its holster.

While Bob and Charley Ford were going through the formality of being jailed and tried for the murder, they consoled themselves that this was not such a hard way to earn the ten-thousand-dollar reward which had been offered for the capture of Jesse James, alive or dead. However, though they were given the governor's pardon they had been promised, they received only five hundred dollars. Nobody has ever been sure what happened to the rest of that reward money.

2 Henry Plummer

THE morning of January 10, 1864, dawned bright and crisp in Bannack, Montana. In the town jail Sheriff Henry Plummer, tall, dark, very handsome, got up early, shaved, and ordered a heavy breakfast. John X. Beidler, United States deputy-marshal, brought it to him. Plummer ate heartily. It was his last meal.

Within two hours he was to be dead on the scaffold which he himself had built in the name of law and order. John Beidler was to be his hangman.

'Sorry, Hank?' Beidler asked.

'I've lived well,' Plummer replied.

Plummer was a well-educated, dapper son of a wealthy Connecticut family. He was born on July 6, 1837, and matured as a strikingly attractive man.

When only fifteen years old Henry Plummer went to California. A year later, in 1853, he and a partner, Henry Hyer, opened the Empire Bakery in Nevada City, California. It was not odd for young teenagers to hit the wander trail in those frontier days. The West beckoned to many—some to become outlaws and killers, some men of note. A later member of Plummer's gang, Boone Helm, was just a young boy when he fled from his Log Branch, Missouri, home after he had killed a man. The noted Indian scout, Tom Horn, was just fourteen years of age when he left Memphis, Missouri, for Kansas City and employment on the Santa Fe Railroad. The famous Kit Carson ran away from his Howard County, Missouri, home because he did not want to learn harness-making. Kit was just sixteen at the time. The noted peace officer, buffalo hunter, and editor, Bat Masterson, ran away from his Fairfield, Illinois, home on his sixteenth birthday. There are many similar cases.

Henry Plummer was a young man of gentle manners, and had the gift of ingratiating himself with both sexes. Only when he became excited by passion did his savage instincts get the better of him; then he became a demon in human form.

Nevada City was a wild, gold-feverish town during the 1850's; the people cared little about law-enforcement or who was the law. Although only nineteen, in 1856 Henry Plummer was elected marshal of the town. Gold was discovered at Sutter's Mill in 1849 and in 1850 California was admitted to the Union. Gold towns mushroomed overnight. Nevada City was one of them.

Plummer's office as marshal had only a one-year term and during that time he made a name for himself by keeping the rowdy miners from causing trouble in the several mercantile stores and the barber's. Henry frequented the various saloons and bawdy-houses as much as the rest of the citizens so inclined. Towards the end of his first official year he easily won the nomination for another term. However, his activities as a gambler-marshal became so notorious that his supporters dropped him for another candidate. It was just as well, for Henry never would have made it.

In September 1857, before the end of his official term as marshal, Plummer was caught in an intimacy with Mrs. John Vedder by the husband himself and in his own home. Ordered to leave, Plummer promptly shot and killed the man.

John Vedder had friends among the miners. Plummer, arrested and tried for his crime, was found guilty in Nevada City, county seat of Nevada County, and sentenced to ten years in prison. Soon afterwards a new trial was granted on the grounds that three of the jurors were biased. In April 1858

Henry Plummer was tried in Yuba County. This trial confirmed the original verdict, and Plummer was sent to prison.

The convicted man's friends made no move for several months, but then petitioned Governor John P. Weller to obtain Plummer's release, stating that the prisoner was suffering from a severe case of 'galloping consumption' and did not have long to live. The governor pardoned Plummer. The ex-convict returned to Nevada City, where he got in touch with Henry Hyer and the two opened the Lafayette Bakery.

Restless, he soon sold his interest in the bakery and started for San Francisco, but infatuation for a certain prostitute of Nevada City brought him back.

One thing led to another. Plummer became involved in a bawdy-house fight with a stranger, and struck him on the head. The man recovered, however, so Henry escaped punishment. Shortly thereafter he was involved in a raid of the Wells-Fargo Express office at Washoe, but again escaped conviction because of insufficient evidence. Henry's next step outside the law was the murder of Jim Ryder in a Nevada City bawdy-house. It looked as though Plummer was at the end of his rope, but the resourceful young man bribed the jailer and escaped.

Plummer fled from California to Oregon, throwing off pursuit by sending detailed accounts of the hanging of James Mayfield and Henry Plummer for the murder of Sheriff Blackburn to several California newspapers. All Henry accomplished on the way north was the seduction of a man's wife in Walla Walla, Washington. At Orofino, Idaho, Plummer and a man named Ridgley murdered the owner of a gambling establishment.

Late in 1860 Plummer rode into the mining camp of Lewiston, Idaho, and secured a job at one of the gambling-houses. He quickly impressed the local inhabitants with his skill at both cards and six-guns. A few days after his arrival, Lewiston was given an example of his efficiency with a gun, for a grizzly miner laughed at his mincing way of talking, and the Connecticut Yankee had his gun in hand before the laughter had faded from the man's lips. In fact, the miner died in the street with his death-grin frozen on his face. He was the first of Henry Plummer's victims in this locality, though the fast-

THE PACIFIC EXPRESS COMPANY

OFFERS SPECIAL INDUCEMENTS

To all SHIPPERS for the Safe and Rapid Transportation of Money, Valuables, Parcels, and Freight to all Points in the United States, Canada and Foreign Countries.

SAFETY! DESPATCH! RELIABILITY! FAST TIME! PROMPT DELIVERY!

Bill Through to all Important Cities, East, West, North and South. Rates Low as Can be Made.

Operating 40,000 Miles of Railway Lines,

MAKES THROUGH CONNECTIONS WITH

All other RELIABLE EXPRESS COMPANIES, and OPERATES THROUGH CARS between all IMPORTANT POINTS

REACHING DIRECT TO

New York, N. Y.	St. Louis, Mo.	Indianapolis, Ind.	Cairo, Ill.	Dallas, Tex.
Boston, Mass.	St. Joseph, Mo.	Butte City, Mont.	Little Rock, Ark.	Fort Worth, Tex.
Buffalo, N. Y.	Kansas City, Mo.	Omaha, Neb.	Galveston, Tex.	Sherman, Tex.
Philadelphia, Pa.	Atchison, Kan.	Lincoln, Neb.	Shreveport, La.	Palestine, Tex.
Baltimore, Md.	Leavenworth, Kan.	Ogden, Utah.	New Orleans, La.	Keokuk Iowa.
Washington, D. C.	Lawrence, Kan.	Salt Lake City, Utah.	San Antonio, Tex.	Quincy, Ill.
Pittsburgh, Pa.	Topeka, Kan.	Louisville, Ky.	El Paso, Tex.	St. Paul, Minn.
Detroit, Mich.	Denver, Col.	Leadville, Col.	Laredo, Tex.	San Francisco, Cal.
Cincinnati, Ohio.	Des Moines, Iowa.	Memphis, Tenn.	Houston, Tex.	Sacramento, Cal.
Cleveland, Ohio.	Helena, Mont.	Minneapolis, Minn.	Austin, Tex.	San Jose, Cal.
Chicago, Ill.				

AND ALL OTHER CITIES AND IMPORTANT TOWNS.

To Secure Quickest Time. Lowest Rates and Safe Delivery.

ORDER GOODS SHIPPED BY PACIFIC AND UNITED STATES EXPRESS CO'S

The Pacific Express Company proudly offered service to most of the major cities in the East and West promising safe transportation of money and valuables

drawing Yankee was to add many another to his record, each in an abrupt duel or street fight.

Overrun with murderers, robbers, and easy-buck toughs, Lewiston was a ripe plum, ready to be picked by a man with vision and brains. The gold-laden stages made scheduled runs between the various towns and all mail and business money was transported by means of mounted messengers. Besides this rich cargo individual miners with their bulging pokes made frequent trips into town.

With his guns riding low on the hips and ready to bellow death, Henry easily organized the local hoodlums. There was no legal authority to restrain them, so the gang killed and looted in broad daylight.

Plummer never appeared in these brazen robberies and murders, but kept his gunmen loyal to him by his reputation for meting out sudden death. When one of the puppets stepped out of line the sentence was quick execution from Plummer's smoking pistols. He could kill without batting his cold, steel-blue eyes. He continued to operate a faro layout, posing as a fairly respectable citizen, and few realized that he was pulling the strings which operated a vicious outlaw gang.

The roads in and out of Lewiston became death-traps. The heavily laden gold trains were easy targets for the masked gunmen who attacked swiftly, and the Lewiston stagecoach was held up time after time.

In desperation the lawful Lewistonians organized a Vigilante Committee ready to ride out on a moment's notice to answer the gang's challenge. Henry Plummer was one of the first to join the Vigilantes. He made robust speeches from street corners demanding quick justice for the thieves. The fact that he himself had gunned down several men in the saloons and streets of Lewiston was not to his discredit, for it was known that most of his victims had been ruffians, anyway. Gunfighting at that time and place was regarded as a duel of honour, and Plummer's occupation, gambling, was a highly respectable profession.

It became quickly apparent that it would take more than the Vigilantes to establish law in Lewiston and the surrounding mining camps. As if by schedule the stagecoaches carrying gold out of the mining town were robbed regularly, the masked riders appearing in such numbers that the guards dropped their guns, since to put up any kind of fight meant suicide. The killers also dominated the mining camps. At the first hint of opposition they poured dozens of shots into everything that moved.

The Vigilantes attempted to fight fire with fire, but all their plans seemed to backfire. When the lawmen rode out to intercept the thieves, they themselves were ambushed; when they returned to their homes, assassins picked them off in their own living-rooms or drew them into gunfights in the streets. It was soon apparent that there was a leak, but nobody suspected Plummer as the finger man who ordered the murder of the Vigilantes and briefed the outlaws on every effort made for reform.

Plummer's greed and open plundering finally killed the town itself. With its goldfields running barren, and sudden death the price for working the hills surrounding the bullet-riddled city, the gold workers moved away to seek wealth in Elk City or Florence. Lewiston became a dead town, its cafés empty, its streets whipped by mournful, howling winds. But Plummer and his men followed the gold trail, and stage robberies were resumed.

Plummer's nimble fingers went right on dealing faro in the new location, his handsome, sober face masking his deadly secret, his quick eyes and sharp ears picking up every shred of information and passing it quickly to the outlaw gang. His raiders were actually responsible for dotting the maps of Idaho and Montana with ghost town after ghost town, for his gunmen soon outnumbered the men working the glittering hills. Mining camps might sprout a few permanent buildings, but soon the miners would move on when fear of the killer mob permeated the fields. Always the bandana killers moved on with them, operating openly.

The migration of honest gold seekers quickly concentrated at Bannack, in the middle of the Montana gold strike. This miners' camp, with temporary tents wallowing in muddy streets, mushroomed. Rambling general stores sprouted among the canvas dwellings, and even a few wooden houses were built.

The gamblers deserted their circus-like tents to build permanent gambling dens in this raw town that was riding the crest of the boom. The miners, tired of being victimized, wore guns and learned to draw swiftly and kill first.

The first real threat to Plummer's empire was a man named Hank Crawford. Jack Cleveland, an old partner-in-crime of Plummer's, had come to Bannack and demanded a cut in Henry's operations. He knew what was going on, for he was well acquainted with Plummer from several years back. On January 14, 1863, Cleveland and Plummer shot it out in Goodrich's saloon. Cleveland was mortally wounded, but no citizen offered to assist him, so great was their fear of the outlaw band. Hank Crawford ran to the saloon when he heard the shot and volunteered to take the wounded man to his own room. Cleveland lived for several hours and during that time he asked Crawford to seek Plummer and obtain some blankets from him. Henry was suspicious of this errand on behalf of Cleveland, and astonished that he was still alive.

'Did he tell you anything?' he asked Crawford.

'About what?'

'Oh, about his past life or his acquaintances or his friends.'

'Cleveland has no friends. I will see to his burial myself. That is the least another human being can do for a down-and-out.'

With that Crawford walked from the room. An astute man, Crawford noticed Plummer's anxiety, and began to watch the man closely. The rough but honest miners listened with interest whenever Crawford voiced his suspicions of corruption in Plummer, and in very short order elected him the first sheriff of Bannack.

As sheriff, Crawford was called to quell a disturbance in a saloon one night and managed to quiet things down. Suddenly a man approached him and wanted to know what was going on. The sheriff told him it was none of his business, but the man refused to keep a civil tongue.

'I dare you to take off your guns and tackle me.'

Crawford saw that the stranger wore no gunbelt so he discarded his own and stepped up. Instantly the antagonizer drew a hidden pistol, but Crawford was too quick and disarmed him. Plummer joined the man, and it would have gone badly with Crawford if Hank and Harry Phleger hadn't appeared and escorted him to his home. The whole affair was a plot to assassinate the new sheriff, for outside the saloon a pair of Plummer's men lay in wait, armed with double-barrelled shotguns.

Hank Crawford, a butcher by trade, went frequently to Deer Lodge to purchase cattle. When the appointed time for one such trip arrived, the treacherous Plummer started ahead of Crawford. Some unexpected business detained Crawford, who sent an assistant in his place. Once more thwarted, and almost sure that the sheriff knew his secret, Plummer was determined that Crawford must die.

The climax came one day when Crawford stepped into a restaurant for a cup of coffee. Learning that Crawford was unarmed, the outlaw chief rushed to the butcher's, armed with a double-barrelled shotgun. It looked bad for the sheriff. At the last minute, however, Frank Ray, a friend of the sheriff, levelled his weapon at Plummer and fired. The ball broke his right arm.

Although Plummer never managed to kill Crawford, the shooting affair accomplished the outlaw's desire. Hank well knew that sooner or later he would fall victim to ambush lead. He tossed in his badge and returned to his home in Wisconsin.

Plummer recovered from the wound, but his gun arm was useless. Concealing the fact that he no longer could manage a gun effectively with his right hand, he practised day and night until he could draw and fan off shots with his left hand. He knew if his secret got out his own men would probably gun him down, but he had to entrust the gang's leadership to one of his more deadly gunfighters, Boone Helm.

Helm was a sulky, depraved killer whose past was whispered in the bars even among his own confederates. He was a native of Log Branch, Missouri, near the home of the James boys, and, like Billy the Kid, he had committed his first murder when a boy, stabbing a friend to death. He eluded a sheriff's posse by going to Salt Lake City, where he was a hired killer for a while, but forced to flee. At Florence, Idaho, he shot down an unarmed man, but he bribed a jailer and escaped as his gallows was being erected. In San Francisco he lived high, throwing gold about recklessly until he murdered a man in a fight over a woman and had to run once more. Next he was known in Oregon, where he was branded a cannibal. Hired as a guide for six men trekking from Grande Ronde Valley, Oregon, to Salt Lake City, he started the trip in the dead of winter. Within a few weeks, ripped by blizzards and stinging rain, the group became played out, until only Helm and E. Burton survived. Burton cracked after their provisions ran out, when they were trapped in the frozen wilderness, and committed suicide in the Snake River country in Idaho. Helm then butchered Burton's body as he would have a steer's and carried the legs of the luckless traveller in a bag slung over his shoulder, until he staggered into a Blackfoot Indian along the trail.

With Crawford out of the way, Plummer became a candidate for Crawford's abandoned job. The election was an outrage, for Plummer's truc colours were now known to most of the miners, yet his outlaw band swung enough weight—by their number and open intimidations—to elect him sheriff. As soon as he had pinned on the badge, the tough but helpless citizens were ready to leave Bannack, for terror and death became the order of the day.

Plummer's reign was short-lived, however, for a sensational gold strike at Alder Gulch sent the miners scampering. Plummer was left ruling a ghost town. He moved on to Virginia City, Montana, a boisterous city of gold and liquor and gunsmoke.

Most of the population of Virginia City was too busy getting rich to worry about civic affairs, so Henry Plummer got a tight grip on the vote of the boom town, threw off his guise as a gambler, and became a full-time gang chief. His more respectable-looking hoodlums were appointed judges, sentencing according to Plummer's instructions and enriching themselves on fines. Clerks in every large business were on the Plummer payroll, and his most proficient gunfighters wore the stars of deputy-sheriffs, taking their orders from Boone Helm.

More open than ever in his threats and blackmail, Henry Plummer tried to get the choicest plum of all—an appointment as United States deputy-marshal. But here the lawman Nathaniel Langford dared to testify against his character, and he did not win the appointment.

The lack of mail service between Virginia City and the nearest express office at Salt Lake City, five hundred miles away, gave Plummer his best criminal opportunity. Money had to be carried across the country by private messenger—and Plummer controlled a clerk in almost every office where the money was handled.

There was a stageline between Virginia City and the once roaring Bannack, which was now but an intermediary post. At each end of the line Plummer had agents, keeping him supplied with information on shipments of gold. Gunmen ravaged the line, their smoking guns dealing death to anyone who resisted them. When the stages were carrying anything worth stealing, a Plummer agent marked the stage. Other agents noted the mark and passed the word along. In the hills, Plummer's raiders waited in their hideouts, and, when a messenger dashed in with the warning, masked riders swept down to the highway, killed or threatened passengers, and carried off everything of value.

The Plummer men wore only moustaches and side-whiskers, which were somewhat out of fashion in this era of full beards. They had a special hand-clasp and used the password 'innocent' as further identification.

Plummer was sheriff of Virginia City and Bannack at the same time and, whenever he received word of a holdup, he canvassed the saloons and dives, gathering a heavily armed posse and giving chase dramatically—but he never caught any gunmen. Once a driver eagerly told the posse he could make positive identification of the killers if he ever saw them again.

'You sure you'll know these men when you see them?' Plummer asked.

'Sure.'

'You come with me,' Plummer told the driver.

They rode out of earshot of the remainder of the posse.

'You made a mistake,' Plummer told the driver.

He drew swiftly and blasted the unsuspecting driver from the saddle. Then he fired several more shots into the hills. The posse converged on the spot and found Plummer standing beside the dead man.

'They ambushed us as we came over that rise,' he said. 'A couple of 'em headed south.'

He mounted his horse and, leaving a man beside the dead driver, led the posse off on a wild-goose chase across the hills.

Others who believed they could identify the robbers died the same way. Incredibly, even Plummer's bitterest enemies still failed to realize he was the man who was calling every shot for the outlaws.

But his luck was running out. Suspicion was first confirmed in the minds of his enemies when he himself held up a young miner named Tilden who was carrying a considerable amount of gold dust—too much for Plummer to be able to resist. Returning to town, Tilden sought out several friends.

'Damn if that masked man didn't look uncommon like Hank Plummer,' he told them.

A few days later Plummer received word that a party was leaving Virginia City with a heavy load of gold. He sent out two of his deadliest deputies, Dutch John Wagner and Steve Marshland, to intercept the party.

'Wipe 'em out,' he commanded.

This time, as the gold train rode past, Dutch John squeezed off a shot and missed. Warned, the riders whirled their horses and jumped for cover. The afternoon burst alive with gunfire. Dutch John fell first, then Marshland was knocked flat with a slug. The two gunfighters dragged themselves to their horses and made their getaway—but not before they had been recognized.

News of the attack by two of Plummer's deputies spread through the mining camp.

'So Plummer's at the bottom of all this trouble!'

People quickly recalled that one of Plummer's men, George Ives, had been hanged at Nevada City on December 21, 1863, for the murder of a young miner named Nick Tbalt near Alder Gulch, the area of the great gold strike.

'Plummer was responsible for Tbalt's death!' was the cry now. 'Plummer did this too!'

The anti-Plummer faction leaped upon the rumours, fired the entire city with Plummer hatred. On January 4, 1864, two thousand armed miners stormed through the streets of Bannack. Fortunately for Plummer he was out of town, but two of his deputies, Red Yager and G. W. Brown, were caught near Stinkingwater Valley.

'Hank Plummer is sheriff around here,' these deputies protested, 'and we're his assistants. We're the only legal peace officers in the Territory. You got no authority for hangin' or tryin'.'

The mob-crazy Vigilantes hauled Yager and Brown to the nearest tree to hang them without any trial. Begging for mercy, Red Yager confessed to several murders, and reeled off the names of a dozen Plummer gunmen who had worn badges.

'Plummer's the leader!' cried Yager. 'He's the one you want!'

It did no good. They threw a noose around Yager's neck and hauled him off the ground. His neck snapped and he jerked at the end of the rope. Brown was next.

The crowd turned its attention towards the remaining outlaw deputies. Several of them had fled when the mob first gathered, but others were trapped in the raging town. Volley after volley of heavy bullets were fired through the town in such a haphazard manner that it was a wonder half the citizens were not killed. Screams of panic-stricken children and terrified women intermingled with those of horses struck by bullets.

When the smoke finally cleared the Plummer gang had been disposed of.

The Vigilantes rode out of town, tracked down Henry Plummer, and dragged him back to his own jail. From his cell in Bannack Plummer wrote to his family in Connecticut:

> This territory has been taken over by Confederate bushwhackers and, although I'm the duly elected sheriff, I'm about to be lynched because of my loyalty to the Union.

Plummer was only twenty-six years old, and his crime career had lasted only three or four years—but they were bloody years. He himself had killed fifteen men, and his subordinates had committed more than a hundred murders at his command.

Sitting there waiting for Beidler to swing open the cell gate and lead him to the scaffold, Plummer probably reflected on those wasted years. Had he used his brains in legitimate fields, he may well have prospered. Plummer had a keen mind. He had successfully operated several bakeries in Nevada City, and doubtless had the energy and imagination to have explored the rich mining possibilities of the time and place had he so chosen to do. But once he had tasted the power and the comfort of the rich outlaw's life it was impossible for him to turn back.

'Get going,' Beidler said. He twisted the key in the lock and pulled open the iron gate.

Plummer walked through and looked around.

'Damnedest thing,' he muttered. 'I'm the one that built this jail.'

'Yes, and the scaffold as well,' put in Beidler.

Out in the bright morning the crowd of miners he had

victimized stood waiting. He mounted the scaffold. Then his nerve cracked. As he stared through the loop of the noose tears streamed out of his eyes, and he began to beg.

'Don't hang me. For God's sake, don't hang me!' he cried, dropping to his knees.

Here from the scaffold he now revealed for the first time that he had a young wife in Connecticut.

'She doesn't know anything about all this. Give me another chance!' he begged.

Beidler hauled him to his feet and again slipped the noose around his neck. He plunged through the trap, his body snapped at the end of the rope, and a sharp crack echoed through Bannack's streets, writing an end to Plummer's career.

On January 14, 1864, just four days after Plummer was executed, Boone Helm was arrested while trying to flee the territory. His trial was quick. Vainly he protested against the charges hurled at him, but the jury laughed in his face. They found him guilty of murder and robbery, and the sentence was immediate hanging at Virginia City.

Calmly Helm cracked jokes as he was led to the box scaffold. He was not afraid to die, but stood coolly to the end. As he stepped up on the box he turned and bellowed his last defiant words:

'Every man for his principles! Hurrah for Jeff Davis! Let 'er rip!'

The executioner jerked the box from under his feet, and the last of Plummer's gang was gone.

In the months that followed, Plummer's young wife arrived in Virginia City and Bannack, interviewed miners and leafed through the scanty records, seeking some confirmation that her husband had been lynched by Confederate sympathizers as he had written her. Feeling for her sake ran high, and many people were beginning to think the hanging of Henry Plummer had been a mistake, anyway. But finally even his wife admitted her husband had been a blackguard and that he had been executed in justice. The people were kind to Mrs. Plummer and afforded her every comfort, well knowing she had nothing to do with her husband's depravity. History, too, has been kind to her, for no account has been kept of her moves. She dropped completely from sight after her tragic visit to Montana.

3 King Fisher

THE sign at the intersection of the two dusty roads reads:

THIS IS KING FISHER'S ROAD—
TAKE THE OTHER ONE

'Who's King Fisher?' one of the riders asked. 'What in hell right has he got posting a county road?'

The other rider looked at his companion sceptically.

'Road leads past his ranch, so he made a private road out of it.'

'How come? What does he think he is, a real king?'

'If you don't know who King Fisher is, you'll find out pretty quick. That is, if you're fixing to stay in Texas.'

King Fisher was one of those colourful characters who strode majestically across the stage of time, performed his act, and made his abrupt departure. Although christened John King Fisher, Junior, posterity will recognize him as just plain King Fisher. He was a product of the Border, a Texan, who as a boy was thrown upon his own resources amid surroundings which in no small measure were responsible for the life into which he drifted.

King Fisher was born in Kentucky in 1859, when storm clouds were gathering between the States and war was imminent. The lad was too small to remember his father as a fighting man of the Confederacy. After the close of the war father and son were more like strangers. The war had dealt harshly with all connected with the Lost Cause, and John King Fisher, Senior, found that only desolation awaited him. He left Kentucky and arrived in Fort Worth, Texas.

Fisher Senior was such a hater of Yankees that he soon found himself in trouble when he tangled with the Reconstruction element in Fort Worth. Hot words passed between Fisher and an ex-soldier of the Union, which led to an exchange of bullets instead of words, and when the smoke cleared young Fisher found himself an orphan. The teenage boy was destitute, a stranger in a strange land. All he could do was accept odd jobs from various ranchers in and around Goliad until impatient feet got him on the move again.

Not far from Goliad young Fisher asked Rancher White for a job.

'What might your name be, son?'

'They call me John King Fisher.'

White burst into a loud laugh.

'That's shore a plumb fittin' name for you, lad. You shore as hell look like one of them kingfisher birds. You are built like a colt, split more than halfway up.'

From that day until his death the lad was known only as King Fisher.

Young Fisher soon became accustomed to his new home. Rancher White became 'Uncle White' and the missus became 'Aunt Lou'. Second to the Whites' home King found the ranch of Charlie Vivian the most attractive. The boy had taken a great liking to Sarah Vivian, Charlie's pretty daughter, and always managed to spend some time there.

In 1870 a number of ranchers around Goliad decided to move to the Nueces Strip, an area of land a hundred miles wide and three hundred miles long, situated between the Nueces and the Rio Grande Rivers, inhabited by wanted men from every State in the Union. King Fisher requested permission to accompany Uncle White, who was elected captain of the wagon train, but was turned down.

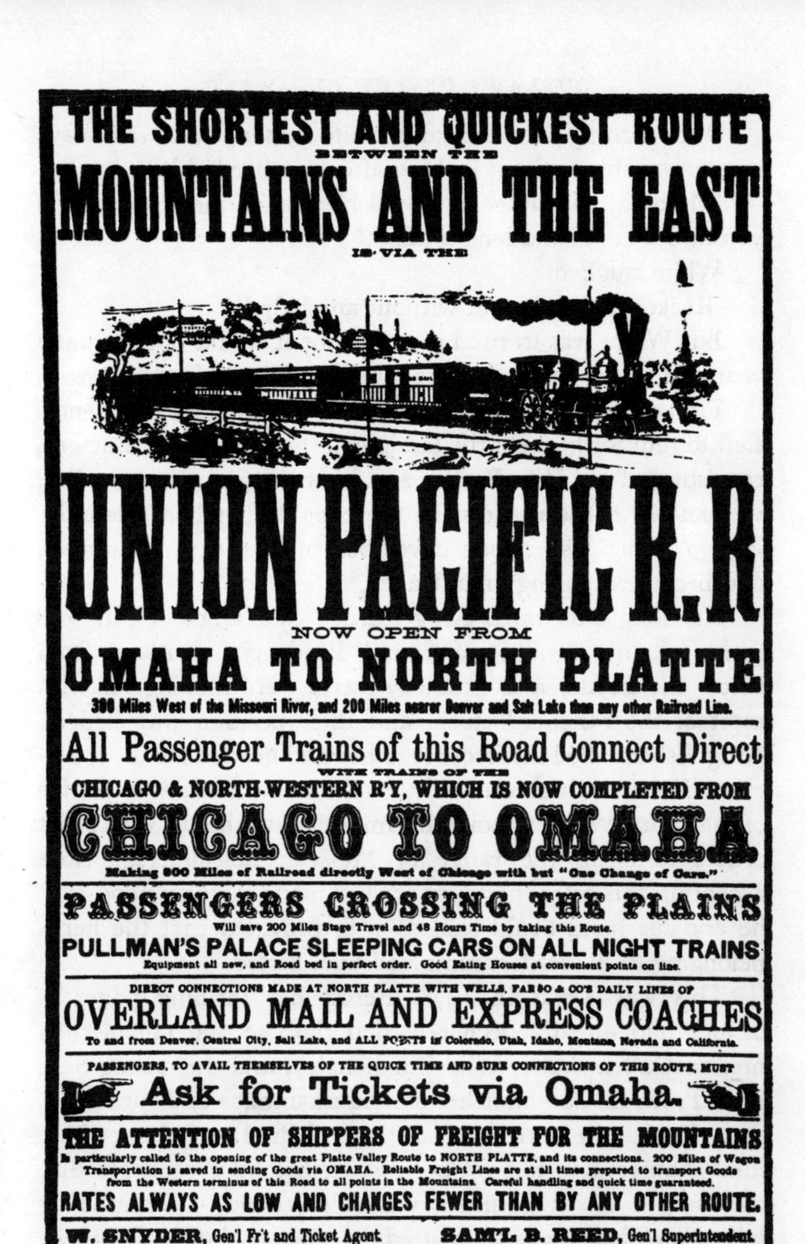

Speed, convenience, and low rates were stressed by the expanding Union Pacific even in the early days of railroading

'We're going into a man's country, son, and we'll have enough trouble without looking after another kid.'

'Might be that later on you'll be needin' me, Unc, and if you do I'll come and lend a hand.'

White laughed.

'Reckon I'll make out without any help.'

But White was to rue his words, for it would not be many years before he was in desperate need of King's deadly guns.

Fisher did not remain idle after the departure of his friends. Left to shift for himself, the lad joined the ranks of the Burtons, consisting of old Wes Burton and his two sons, Wes and Bill, well-known cattle rustlers. In the capable hands of the elder Burton, King Fisher soon developed into an expert gunman, and became the gang's real leader.

Not long afterwards King learned that Uncle White was facing chaotic conditions around Pendencia. Outlaws from below the Border and runaway slaves were making off with most of the ranchers' stock, and their position was critical. King Fisher called his forces together and headed for the settlement. His arrival soon turned the tables on the outlaws. Justice of the Peace White appointed him a deputy-sheriff, with strict orders to clean the range of Mexican marauders. Before accepting this offer, however, Fisher made it understood that he and his band could raid at will, provided that the herds belonging to the settlers remained unmolested.

This was Texas in 1878. Across her thrilling pages of history had already been recorded the rise and fall of such men as Cullen Baker, Wild Bill Longley, and the daring Sam Bass. From its Commanche-infested mountains and sprawling, dusty Panhandle were to come others of equal note, those whose final chapters had not yet been written. John Wesley Hardin, the king of Texas gunmen, was still around, the blustering killer Ben Thompson yet strutted the walk, as did the Clements and the vicious assassin Killing Jim Miller, one of the most proficient Western professors in the science of homicide.

Already John King Fisher was truly king of Texas. His

roaring ivory-handled, silver-plated revolvers had put thirteen men in their graves. He had swaggeringly made cattle-rustling and horse-theft a booming business. Once he actually frustrated the Texas Rangers to a point where a captain released a prisoner because he was convinced the cause of justice in Texas was dead.

Despite his outrageous conceit, less is known about King Fisher than of the gunmen who followed him. Yet he was one of the most fantastic dudes of the day, and openly bragged of killing a baker's dozen white men 'not counting greasers'.

In his book about early law and order in the Lone Star State, *A Texas Ranger*, N. A. Jennings says:

> Fisher was about twenty-five years old at the time (1876) and the most perfect specimen of manhood and frontier dandy and desperado I ever met.
>
> He was tall, beautifully proportioned and exceedingly handsome. He wore the finest clothing procurable, but all of the picturesque, Border, dime-novel kind.

Fisher's broad-brimmed white Mexican sombrero was profusely ornamented with gold and silver lace and had a golden snake for a band. His fine buckskin Mexican short jacket was heavily embroidered with gold. Beneath it, a brilliant crimson silk sash was wound about his waist. His shirt was of the finest and thinnest linen, and was usually worn open at the throat, a silk handkerchief knotted loosely about the wide collar. At his hips swung two shining pistols, their pearl handles filed with notches, their plated silver barrels glistening. His boots were of top-grade leather, tooled with careful precision, their high heels cut perfectly. From the point of each silver spur dangled a silver bell.

This flashy eyeful was further set off by *chaperojos*—leather chaps to protect the trouser legs during a ride through brush or while herding cattle. Fisher had killed the animal from which the hide was peeled and had had these chaps especially made.

King had spotted his future breeches one afternoon in Northern Texas while he and some of his bawdy friends were attending a circus. The gang literally kidnapped the circus, holding the owners and spectators at gunpoint while Fisher killed the animal, strapped its carcass to a horse, and rode off. A few days later Fisher appeared in those famous chaps—made from the skin of a Royal Bengal tiger and decorated with gold and buckskin fringe.

Fisher was as deadly a shot with his left hand as with his right, and even today he is considered to have been one of the most remarkable pistoleers that ever lived. He was an equally fine horseman, and his favourite mount was a lemon-coloured palomino stallion with cream mane and tail.

There were few Texans who did not know, or were not at least familiar with, the striking tiger-chapped gunman from Pendencia Creek, in Dimmit County. When he rode—or when he relaxed at his little ranch—he was surrounded by forty or fifty plunderers, cattle rustlers, freebooters, gunfighters, and holdup men, all of them living off booty.

Jennings, when a member of the Texas Rangers, came in close contact with the Beau Brummel killer and had reason to know Fisher's frustrating effect on the law. Once Jennings' company, under command of Captain Jack McNelly, swept down on Fisher's mob during a rustling venture, rounded them up and rode them into Eagle Pass. The charge against Fisher was murder, and the penalty was a hangman's knot.

A few days later McNelly, while out on a scouting trip, picked up a fresh trail, ran it down, and suddenly found himself face to face with the brigand dandy. McNelly pulled up his horse and reached for his gun.

'Hold up a minute, Captain,' Fisher barked, a smile playing across his lips. 'Me and the boys is out on bail. Twenty thousand dollars, matter of fact. Lots of money. 'Course me or any member of this party can get all the bail we want . . . any time we want it.'

'Very well,' McNelly replied. 'If the people in this section of

Texas want such men as you running all over the country, they're welcome. There's no use working my men day and night for a farce like this.'

McNelly turned to one of the Rangers who was guarding a handful of prisoners whom the patrol was escorting to the Eagle Pass jail.

'Turn 'em loose,' he ordered.

McNelly and his group whirled and rode off, leaving the arrogant chieftain behind. After that Fisher held the entire region in the palm of his two deadly hands. Anybody who refused to make bond for one of his hoodlums was a marked man, and any man who objected to the rule of gunsmoke and hell-raising faced the same fate.

Dimmit County became a thieves' hideaway. The Texas Rangers had a booklet listing three thousand fugitives from justice who were suspected of having found refuge there, and had rewards on their heads.

King Fisher's rule of terror soon spread to the neighbouring county of Uvalde, where he managed to blackmail himself into the office of deputy-sheriff, but that was his first—and last—mistake, since the badge indirectly led to his death.

Working in his official capacity he had to make a trip to Austin, the State capital, and while there he encountered Ben Thompson, a killer whose reputation was spreading through Southern Texas. These two men exercised and enjoyed a mutual respect. Fisher, the dude killer, and Thompson, the reckless badman, together took on a rather neat cargo of 'tiger sweat', and when they boarded the train for San Antonio they were swaying. Fisher could handle his liquor, but Thompson started an argument with a porter and whipped out his six-gun, waving it under the porter's nose and threatening to kill him.

'Sit down, Ben. Quit makin' a damn fool out of yourself,' said Fisher.

'Supposin' I don't wanna set down?' Thompson snapped. 'Who's gonna make me set down, huh?'

'I told you to sit down and behave yourself, Ben,' Fisher drawled, 'and by God I mean exactly that.'

'And, if I don't—what then?' Thompson persisted.

'In that case, I expect I'd be forced to kill you.'

'By God!' Thompson replied, a bit awed. 'Damned if I don't believe you'd sure do it.'

That was the only time Ben Thompson was ever known to 'back off' from a showdown.

The two intoxicated killers were friendly enough by the time they reached San Antonio. A short time previously Ben Thompson had killed a man named Harris, the owner of the Variety Vaudeville Theatre in this city, and two friends of Harris's, W. H. Sims and Joe Foster, were now operating the gaudy show palace. Thompson drunkenly decided to return, in spite of Fisher's efforts to dissuade him.

'Damned if I don't think you're afraid to go in there with me,' said Thompson.

'Damn your stinkin' hide,' Fisher growled. 'King Fisher ain't afraid to do anything. I just don't see any damn sense in lookin' for trouble, that's all.'

Ben chuckled drunkenly.

'King, I'm gonna see Foster and ask him to bury the hatchet. You don't wanna go? Then I'll go by myself.'

'Bury the hatchet, hell! You're just lookin' for trouble. But I'll side you. Lead the way.'

They weaved through the streets of San Antonio and entered the Variety. Sims met the pair and offered drinks.

Thompson said, 'I'd like to see Foster and talk over the prospects of buryin' the hatchet.'

'I'll go see what he has to say,' Sims told them.

The two desperadoes went upstairs and took seats in a booth. As was later brought out at the inquest, the meeting between Foster and Thompson resulted in a heated argument. Thompson is said to have hurled abusive remarks at both Sims and Foster, while Fisher tried to act as peacemaker. The talk began to cool and Foster and Sims prepared to leave the booth. Then Thompson boisterously announced he was going to 'shoot up the place', and reached for his six-gun.

Fisher wanted no part of the clean-up party, so he called in a Mexican policeman named Coy to help quieten Thompson. Soon the talk got around to the way Thompson had recently killed a rancher named Wilson, and Foster began to glower again.

Thompson was resuming his rosy outlook on life, so he reached across the table to shake hands with Foster.

'You damn thief, I won't shake hands with you!' Foster shouted.

'God damn you, I'm glad you won't!' Thompson growled.

Coy stepped over and placed one hand on his arm, but Thompson shook it off.

'Get out of my way and let me settle this affair with Foster!' he bellowed.

He moved like a rattlesnake, his face red with anger. Leaping across the table, he slapped Foster in the face, then drew his pistol and rammed the barrel into Foster's mouth. Coy managed to pull the gun away, but it roared, the bullet whistling past Foster's ear and splitting the wall.

'God damn you!' Thompson yelled. 'Turn my pistol loose!'

'Stop your brawling!' commanded Coy.

Foster and Sims were trying to slip away when Coy pleaded: 'Don't leave! I need your help!'

Thompson and Fisher arose. Neither had pistols in shooting position, but both Sims and Foster evidently were expecting something else. They jumped to one side, and as they did a salvo of shots rent the air. The volley had come from above and to the left. Both Fisher and Thompson dropped, victims of assassin lead. A scheme of the two arch-conspirators, Sims and Foster, had worked with accuracy, and no proof of their hand in the plot to dispose of their hated enemy, Ben Thompson, was ever unearthed.

When the smoke cleared away Fisher and Thompson lay

dead, side by side, Thompson's arm flung across his dead friend's chest. Thompson had taken five bullets through his head and four through his body. Fisher had been shot thirteen times, one bullet tearing through his left eye directly into the brain.

The *Austin Daily Statesman* described the scene under date of March 12, 1884:

When your reporter reached the scene the two bodies were weltering in blood and laid out side by side, their hair and faces carmined with the life fluid. The stairs leading to the scene of horror were slippery as ice and the walls were stained and the floor tracked with bloody footprints.

Women in the Variety Theatre rushed to the blood-soaked booth screaming: 'Which is Ben? Show me Ben!'

Stories circulated through the city that Thompson had been lured to his death, and on March 13 the *Austin Daily Dispatch* reported:

. . . The general verdict in our city is that Thompson was lured into a trap and brutally assassinated, and that the affair was a well-laid, coolly prepared plan to murder him. The verdict of the coroner's jury is simply prepared to suit the case, and is not sustained by the facts. The evidence given before the jury is unworthy of credence, and was given merely by those who desired Thompson's death. That Thompson came to his death by shots from the pistols of Foster and officer Coy is unworthy of belief. . . .

Regardless of the scorching accusation of the Press, a coroner's jury returned the following verdict:

That Ben Thompson and J. K. Fisher both came to their deaths on the 11th day of March 1884, while at the Vaudeville Theatre in San Antonio, Texas, from the effects of pistol-shot wounds from pistols held in and fired from the hands of J. C. Foster and Jacob S. Coy, and we further find that the said killings were justifiable and done in self-defence in the immediate danger of life.

Austin newspapers continued to harass the city and its jury for returning a verdict which was considered unjustified. The *Austin Daily Dispatch* the same day commented:

> The facts of the case do not bear out this verdict. A reputable gentleman, not a resident of Texas, but who was in San Antonio the night of the shooting, and who saw and conversed with Thompson half an hour before he was shot, says he was informed by a police officer that the police force had orders to kill Thompson on the slightest provocation.
>
> Ben Thompson was killed in San Antonio, and that city is welcome to all the glory there is in such a brutal and cowardly assassination. We had read in history that it was common in Italy and Spain to hire men to commit assassination, but it has been left to San Antonio to inaugurate this hellish business in this country. We hope never to hear anything said about lawlessness in Austin again. There never was, and we trust there never will be, such a cowardly and brutal act committed in this city. San Antonio is alone in this great country where hired assassination is endured and approved by the people and Press, and it is welcome to the glory. No other city in Texas, nor do we believe in this whole land, has a human slaughter-house like this den of hell, the Vaudeville Theatre, or a Press that would palliate and sustain such an infamous place.

Joe Foster, whose leg was riddled in the gun-battle, died eleven days later, after an unsuccessful amputation. He died with his lips sealed.

Coy always denied he had fired any shot in the bloody battle.

On March 13, 1884, Ben Thompson, who had been a major in the Confederate Army, was buried with full military honours while crowds of people thronged to his funeral. King Fisher, the dapper gentleman killer, was carried back to his notorious ranch, there to be buried in the jingling spurs and tiger chaps he had loved.

4 The Reno Brothers

IN THE years which followed the Civil War the mid-western Border States became a lawless frontier, bullet-riddled and ravaged by hordes of men hated by the South as renegades and sought by the North as guerrilla fighters.

Lee's surrender meant nothing to William Clarke Quantrill and his notorious raiders, nor to Bloody Bill Anderson, Arch Clements, Frank or Jesse James. They were men without a country, hunted by Union soldiers and Southern lawmen. For Quantrill the war came to an end only when he died at Wakefield Farm, Kentucky; Bloody Bill died in a hail of .44 slugs in Orrick, Ray County, Missouri; Jesse and Frank James blasted a niche in history with gunfire, as we have seen, but it was just a question of time before they had to stop.

Another member of this scallywag band who was destined to shoot his way into the pages of history was John Reno, the most savage member of the Reno clan. Of the five brothers only one was to make an honest way, Clint Reno, and because he chose to remain on the safe side of the law he was referred to by thc townsfolk as 'Honest Clint'. But he too suffered the stain that the Reno boys of Seymour, Indiana, blotted across the name.

Today John Reno would be termed a juvenile delinquent, and had a court intercepted his career when it began during his eleventh year, he might never have gone so sour. But the

Reno family was not a closely knit one; the boys did not get along well with their father. After the war it was not much better, with Seymour overrun by confidence men who swindled veterans, and armed bands of robbers looting the countryside.

John left home when he was eleven, riding one of his father's best horses, and this sullen parent was concerned more over the loss of the animal than over the disappearance of his son. He promptly dispatched a cousin of John's, James Smith, to catch up with the boy across the Ohio River and bring back the horse. Smith overtook John in Louisville, Kentucky, and offered him a hundred dollars of Mr. Reno's money for the horse.

'Your old man says you can take the money and go any place you want to,' the cousin told him.

'That's fine by me!' was John Reno's quick response.

He accepted the hundred dollars and waved good-bye to Cousin James and the horse. He set out to conquer the world, but soon learned that it took more than guts and a hundred dollars.

He invested part of his funds in a ticket on the river paddle-wheel steamer *Fannie Ballet*, bound for New Orleans. But New Orleans was a city well-versed in sin and with little heart for the wandering stranger, and an eleven-year-old was easy pickings. For one thing, Northern currency was considered 'foreign' and had to be exchanged for local money at a tremendous discount. Reno decided to play it smart, but when he attempted to pass off the Northern money in a store, he was caught and had to pay a five-dollar bribe to a police officer to keep out of jail. In disgust he headed up-river to Memphis to visit kinsfolk.

In Memphis Reno's relatives provided him with a few lessons in skullduggery. A drunken lot, they were masters in the art of thumb-and-knee fighting and the use of the knife. While he was with them his uncle became involved in a street brawl during which he carved up his opponent.

The boy decided to take another fling at New Orleans, so he worked his way back to the city and got a job unloading cotton from the river-boats tied up at the sprawling levee. He landed another job on the river-boat *John C. Fremont.* Twenty-five miles out of New Orleans, Reno realized the work was back-breaking and offered little pay. He jumped ship and found himself penniless in an alien land along the banks of the Mississippi, where Jim Lane and John Brown were in the midst of a bitter struggle against the so-called 'Border Ruffians' of Kansas. In these days prior to the Civil War anti-Yankee feeling was intense in this area.

John Reno trudged twelve or thirteen miles up-river and hid in a wood-yard. When the steamer *Ingomar* pulled in that night to replenish its wood supply, he slipped aboard and stowed away, but was thrown off near Vicksburg. He set out afoot, arriving in that city tired and hungry. On the water-front he discovered a gang of river-raftsmen about to go to breakfast, so he stepped into line and enjoyed his first meal in twenty-four hours.

He remained in Vicksburg four or five days then got a job on the *Southern Belle.* He earned twenty-six dollars a month. Then he signed on a 'coasting trade' boat as deckhand at a dollar a day and arrived at New Orleans twenty-six days later.

After a few months of living as a scavenger and dock tramp, he headed for home. He appeared in Seymour in dirty, ragged trousers and a tattered shirt, full of tall tales of his adventures along the Mississippi. But his pockets were empty, and the greeting was cold.

Reno took care of both problems. He helped himself to eleven hundred dollars hidden in the Reno house and went to Rockford, Illinois. Having no confidence in banks, he deposited the money with a cousin for safe-keeping. A few days later he discovered his relative had 'lost' about three hundred dollars. In the ensuing argument the cousin informed the police that John had stolen over a thousand dollars from his parents and

Reno was arrested for theft. The young burglar escaped and headed for Indianapolis, arriving just as the news was received that Fort Sumter had been fired upon. The city was wild with patriotic excitement, the streets were decked with flags, and the fifteen-year-old Reno enlisted in the Union Army.

He was sent almost immediately to the front and fought in the battle of Rich Mountain, and afterwards was reassigned as assistant wagon-master, running military supplies between Huntsville and Beverly.

By now John Reno was a tough customer. He was arrested for stealing a lieutenant's wallet, but a court martial exonerated him. Reassigned to Norfolk, Virginia, he deserted. Fourteen days later he was picked up and locked in the guardhouse. With some of the money rifled from the lieutenant's wallet the wily youngster bribed his guard and found freedom once more.

Now officially a deserter, young Reno nevertheless continued to assist in the war effort by inducing young men to join the Army for pay. In those days of the Civil War this practice was called 'bounty jumping'. If a wealthy young man was drafted into service, Reno would offer to find a substitute who would be willing to take his place for a price. Working on a percentage basis, Reno found this a good racket, and he enlisted most of his substitute soldiers from his home town of Seymour.

He rode into town one day and saw that an old friend, George Mace, had been arrested for stealing a horse. Reno edged into the crowd to get a good look at what was going on, and the officers nabbed him. Mace, who was as unprincipled as Reno, implicated his friend, and a mob stormed the jail, dragging Reno to the railroad yards where they tied his hands behind his back, threw a rope over a branch, and then strung him up repeatedly. Reno was jerked from the ground, twisting and gasping, dropped back, jerked again, over and over, while his captors tried to make him confess the theft of a horse. Amid the howling townspeople, most of whom were getting drunker by the moment, he continued to deny any role in the horse-stealing. When he went limp, the drunken mob left him for dead, but Reno was only playing 'possum.

Reno left town, bitter and ripe for a total plunge into lawlessness. Although the next few years in his anti-social career are vague, it is known that he fought with the Border gangs and ran with the marauders. But it was not until the night of October 6, 1866, that he is next pinpointed by historians. On that night an Adams Express Company train was boarded and robbed.

Train robbery was a new thing in those days. Even the James boys, the Youngers, and the Daltons were still young in the profession of armed robbery. So Reno's attack on the train attracted nation-wide attention.

The train had been boarded in the dark forest a few miles outside Seymour by two masked men who crept along the tops of the cars until they reached the car which held the safe. Carefully swinging down between, they ripped through the door and blackjacked the messenger in charge. Then they laboriously shoved the great safe across the floor of the car, tumbled it through the door, rifled the small express safe of sixteen thousand dollars, and pulled the bell cord.

The train slowed to a stop, and the two robbers slipped off into the darkness waving at the driver.

'All right, go ahead!'

The train rumbled off into the night. Several miles later the conductor discovered the unconscious messenger and the looted safe.

Back up the track, the Reno gang had been waiting when the 'through' safe was dumped from the car into the bushes lining the edge of the tracks. They dragged it off the right-of-way. Reno and his assistant walked back down the line, after jumping from the train, and went to work on the big strongbox. Before they could crack it the robbery was discovered, and law officers from the train had started back after them. The gang had to relinquish the safe and its thirty-five-thousand-dollar treasure.

Since the rail detectives had no idea who the masked men were, they interrogated the passengers. One named George Kinney told the officers he thought he could recognize some of the bandits, and a few nights later, when Kinney answered a knock on the door, he was shot dead by a mysterious stranger.

The local townsfolk suspected that the train robbery and the murder of George Kinney had been the work of John Reno, his three brothers, and a man named Frank Sparks. Sparks, John and one of his brothers, Simeon, were arrested and jailed at Lawrenceburg, Indiana. Several days later they were removed to the Brownston jail.

'What happens now?' Simeon asked his brother.

'Don't worry,' John answered.

Within a few days Reno was out under bail—for a thousand dollars less than the amount stolen from the train. The three men were returned to Seymour, where the authorities agreed that evidence against them was far from substantial.

'They'll make a mockery of the court if we try them on what we've got,' the sheriff lamented.

This incident was quickly obscured by a new train robbery on another Adams car which was rifled in exactly the same manner and almost at the same spot, a few miles outside Seymour. Suspicion naturally centred on the Renos, but this time they were innocent, for the second Adams car burglary was the work of two other local boys, Walter Hammond and Michael Colleran. Hammond made a clean getaway with the loot, but he went calling on Reno's girl friend one night with his pockets bulging.

'We'll be rich,' he told her. 'Let's get away from here. Go some place and settle down. Reno's no good.'

The girl was easily swayed, but as she and Hammond were leaving John and Frank Reno stepped out of the shadows.

'You goin' some place, Walt?' John asked.

Hammond stopped cold. The girl screamed and ran inside. The two Renos set upon Hammond and beat him. He tried to break free, but Frank caught him around the chest, and John lashed out, his fist crashing into Hammond's face. The luckless robber dropped forward.

'We better go,' John said. 'We'll make the most of this.'

The two Renos walked to the sheriff's office. The sheriff looked up from his desk.

'Everybody's talking about Frank here and me holdin' up the Adams car the other night,' said John. 'You want the man that done it, he's down the street. Money's still in his pockets.' He smiled and added, 'We nailed him for ya, Sheriff.'

Hammond and Colleran were convicted and given long sentences in the Indiana State Penitentiary.

By now John Reno had lured three of his four brothers into a life of crime. Simeon was out of jail, Frank was well indoctrinated, and William had played a role in the first Adams car robbery and the murder of George Kinney.

Early in the spring of 1867, while his three brothers remained in Seymour, John and a friend, Volney Elliott, rode down to Daviess County, Missouri, soon to experience not only the Reno robbery technique, but, two years later, that of the Jesse James gang. The county seat of Gallatin was a busy and flourishing little town. Reno picked the county treasurer's office to rob that mild April afternoon. The robbery was carried off with ease for the treasurer was alone in his office, which was on the far side of the court-house. Reno and Elliott simply walked in and at pistol point relieved the official of twenty-two thousand dollars in cash—a brazen robbery that sent a thrill of excitement all over the land.

A message was sent to the Pinkerton Detective Agency in Kansas City and was, in turn, relayed to Seymour. As John Reno rode into his home town two Pinkerton men stepped from the pavement and grabbed the bridle of his horse.

'John Reno?' one of them inquired.

'That's me,' Reno swaggeringly answered. 'What the hell is the meaning of this and who are you?'

'We're Pinkertons and you're under arrest,' the officers

said. 'Get down from that horse!' Both Pinkertons drew their pistols and covered John.

'What for?' Reno demanded.

'Holdup. City treasurer in Gallatin. Let's go.'

Reno was returned to Missouri for trial, and his sins were paraded as the State presented its evidence. The judge sentenced him to twenty-five years in the State Penitentiary at Jefferson City.

Most people regarded John Reno as the brains of the Indiana train robbery gang, and thought that with him in jail things would quieten down. But the Renos were just getting started.

A few weeks after John Reno began serving his twenty-five years, a Jefferson, Madison, and Indianapolis train came to a stop at a refuelling and watering-station in the little town of Marshfield. In the dimly lighted wooden coaches the passengers sprawled in fitful sleep. The driver swung down from the cab, lantern swinging from one hand, an oilcan in the other, whistling softly to himself, and he started to make his customary inspection while the tender replenished the wood supply. The shadows moved behind the driver as he held up his lantern. The barrel of a heavy pistol crashed across the top of his head.

Unaware that a drama of violence was unfolding on the other side of the train, the fireman clambered down his ladder to the ground, and a fist smashed into his face from out of the darkness. He reeled backward, and a gun-butt felled him from behind. One of the masked men dropped him beside the driver and stood over both with his gun drawn and the hammer back.

The wood handlers stood like statues, their hands thrust above their heads, while a second masked bandit held a gun on them. The rest of the robbers went to work uncoupling the express car from the passenger coaches, and the engine throttle was slowly pulled open. The engine and express car began to grind down the tracks.

Inside the express car, the messenger sat dozing and rocking with the gentle sway of the train. Beside him sat two old-fashioned safes which contained more than a hundred thousand dollars assigned to banks in New York. As the engine rattled down the tracks, the door behind the messenger was suddenly split wide open with a fire axe. The messenger stared as the door burst open in a shower of splinters, and the masked robbers rushed upon him, slamming him back against the wall and beating him insensible. One of the masked men threw him out of the car and over an embankment.

With axes, the robbers easily shattered the locks of the two safes and gathered up the cash and bonds, then worked their way across the tender into the locomotive.

'Okay,' one of them said. 'Slow it down.'

A mile north of Seymour the thieves abandoned the engine and disappeared into the darkness.

It was a clean sweep. The authorities strongly suspected the Reno gang, but how to capture them was a problem. The Pinkertons followed the trail by tracing the stolen bonds and uncovered some of the loot in Syracuse, New York, still more in Canada. Finally a detective located Frank, Simeon, and William Reno who were living like lords in the town of Sandwich, Ontario. With them was Carl Anderson, and they were all spending money like water. The Pinkertons were helpless, for train robbery was a new offence, not included in the extradition treaty between the United States and Canada.

'All right,' one of the Pinkerton men said. 'Keep an eye on them. They'll slip, and when they do we'll be waiting.'

The cat-and-mouse game of surveillance continued for months, until one day William and Simeon slipped across the border with Carl Anderson, leaving Frank Reno in Canada. The Pinkertons concentrated on the Seymour area in Indiana. They alerted train officials and concealed guards in all express trains.

One night as an express train pulled into the water-station at Brownstown, ten miles south-west of Seymour, masked men appeared, two of them boarding the engine and

ALABAMA LAW.

AN ACT

To Define Train Robbing and Fix a Punishment Therefor.

Section 1. Be it enacted by the General Assembly of Alabama, That, hereafter, any person or persons who may stop or cause to be stopped, or impede or cause to be impeded, or conspire together for that purpose, any locomotive engine or any car or cars, on any railroad in this State, by intimidation of those in charge thereof, for the purpose by force, threats, intimidation, or otherwise, of taking therefrom or causing to be delivered up to such persons or person forcing, threatening, or intimidating, anything of value to be appropriated to his or their own use, shall be guilty of attempting train robbery, and on conviction thereof, shall be punished by ***confinement in the penitentiary for a period of not less than ten or more than thirty years.***

Section 2. Be it further enacted, That any and all persons who may hereafter enter upon any locomotive engine, car or cars, on any railroad in this State, and by threats, the exhibition of deadly weapons or by the discharge of any pistol or gun on, in or near any such engine, car or cars, induce or compel any person or persons on such engine, car or cars to submit and deliver up, or allow to be taken therefrom, or from him or them, anything of value, shall be held guilty of train robbery, and on conviction thereof shall be punished by ***imprisonment in the penitentiary for not less than ten years*** **or may be sentenced to suffer** ***death by hanging*** **in the discretion of the jury trying the case.**

Section 3. Be it further enacted, That this act shall take effect upon its final passage.

Approved February 18, 1895.

W. C. OATES,
Governor.

J. K. JACKSON,
Secretary of State.

The penalties for train robbery became progressively steeper as the outlaws continued to show contempt for law and order ordering the crew off. As they had done in the Marshfield job, they uncoupled the passenger coaches and let the engine slip down the rails for about three miles. So far the robbery was coming off as scheduled, but as they prepared to enter the express car they got a surprise. The door was open. They pushed it aside—and found themselves face to face with the train guards.

'It's a trap!' one of the masked men screamed.

Guns started to blaze. One of the gang crumpled in the doorway, but two of the thieves dragged him out of range while two others blazed away at the guards, who leaped from the train after spreading the alarm.

The reinforcements for the robbers charged up on horses, blazing away at the express car, and they all succeeded in getting away. But one was leaning in the saddle, his leg hanging useless.

Word of the attempted robbery flashed swiftly through the night, and Pinkerton detectives crashed into Volney Elliott's room. They had him cold, for he couldn't run; he was trapped in his chair with a wounded leg.

Shortly afterwards the Pinkertons captured Charles Rosenbaum and Lefty Clinton, two other members of the outlaw gang, near the scene of the crime in Brownstown. These three had never got out of sight of the town. A few nights later this bandit trio were aboard a train *en route* to Seymour for trial. They never made it. Before they were halfway to their destination a red lantern flared ahead on the tracks, and the engine-driver hauled back on his brakes. As the train hissed to its stop, the coaches were filled with men whose faces were draped with red masks.

'My God!' Elliott screamed. 'It's a lynch mob.'

The three prisoners were dragged, screaming, from the train while their guards were held helpless at gun-point in the coaches. From inside the train the passengers could hear the futile yells of the badmen, then sudden silence. The masked Vigilantes disappeared from the train and it lurched ahead. As it rolled by a tree at the edge of the tracks passengers and guards stared mutely through the windows at the three lifeless bodies swaying from a branch.

News of the trio's lynching spread quickly. Simeon and William Reno fled towards the Canadian border. Pinkerton men had by now persuaded Canadian authorities to allow them to arrest Anderson and Frank Reno, on the promise that they would be given a fair trial. Simeon and William, meanwhile, had made it as far as Indianapolis, when the Pinkertons closed their steel trap, and they gave themselves up.

So the Reno gang was finished. Elliott, Rosenbaum, and Lefty Clinton were dead. John Reno was in Missouri State Prison with many years still to serve, and the remaining Reno brothers were in custody, as was Carl Anderson. There remained only the trial.

The Pinkertons still feared the kind of mob violence which had led to the deaths of the other three Reno blacklegs, so they moved the three Renos and Anderson to New Albany, Indiana, fifty miles from the scene of the lynching. The quartet felt safe and even attempted to bribe Sheriff Thomas Fullenlove to let them escape, promising him a part of their hidden booty.

Two hours before daybreak on a frigid December morning, when the community was asleep, a single coach rolled quietly along the tracks into New Albany, its headlights dark.

The *New Albany Daily Ledger* the following day, December 12, 1868, described what happened:

> The entire community was startled—we may say paralysed—at the announcement this morning that the city had been visited by a number of men, supposed to be the Jackson County Vigilance Committee; that the county jail had been forcibly entered and four men, Frank, Simeon, and William Reno, and Charles Anderson, had been hung. . . .
>
> This morning about three o'clock Mr. Luther Whitten, one of the outside guards at the jail, after making his usual rounds, went

into the jail office and sat down by the fire. He had been inside but a few moments when a noise was heard outside and, approaching the door to open it, he was met at the entrance by a party of men, who presented pistols to him, demanding silence on pain of death. Whitten shouted, however, but he was roughly seized by several of the mob and thrown into a corner and informed if he uttered another sound his life would pay the forfeit.

By this time the jail office was filled with men, who commenced searching for the keys to the jail doors. Sheriff Fullenlove, who was sleeping in a room across the hall from the office, heard Whitten shout, and opened the door only to meet a large force of men. Comprehending the situation at once, he rushed down the stairs leading to the basement of the jail residence, for the purpose of giving the alarm. As he went down the stairs, he heard several voices say, 'Shoot down the stairs,' but he was too quick for them, and gained the door leading to the grounds, on the west side of the jail. Here he met another force of armed men, the jail being surrounded with them, and upon seeing pistols pointed at him, exclaimed, 'Gentlemen, don't shoot me, I am the sheriff.' Just as he said this, one of the gang fired, the shot taking effect in the right arm near the elbow, inflicting a very serious and painful wound. The Sheriff shouted, 'Murder! Help!' at the top of his voice, but was soon silenced by a blow over the forehead, from a heavy pistol. He was then taken into the jail hall and placed under guard. The keys of the jail and the cells were demanded of him under threat of death if he refused to deliver them, but Fullenlove, notwithstanding cocked pistols were pointed at his head, told the mob they might kill him before he would give up the keys, or aid them in any way.

All this time, which, however, was but a few moments, men were searching every part of the jail residence for the keys. About a dozen entered the room where Mrs. Fullenlove was in bed, and demanded of her the whereabouts of the keys. Sheriff Fullenlove hearing the demand made of his wife, called to her to let them kill her rather than tell. She did refuse to give them any information, but they succeeded in finding the object of their search in a wash-stand drawer in her room. . . .

The first victim dragged from his cell was Frank Reno, whose piteous cries as the mob placed the fatal noose about his neck are described as most heart-rending. He was held up by some of the mob while the rope was made fast to the iron pillars from the platform around the second tier of the cells. Wm. Reno was the next man brought out, and he was hung alongside his brother and to the same pillar. Simeon Reno was next brought forth from his cell, but he fought the mob with great desperation, knocking one or two of them down before he was overpowered and left suspended between the ceiling and the floor. He was left hanging at the south-west corner of the jail cells, his feet nearly dragging the floor. Charles Anderson, the last victim, was heard to beg for the privilege of praying before the fatal noose was adjusted, but he was told by his relentless enemies to shut up, and soon his body was hanging from the pillar at the south-west corner of the jail cells. . . .

When the mob left the jail they locked the door and carried away the keys, taking Mr. Perrette along with them to the train at the foot of State Street. Mr. Perrette informs us that the train was composed of two passenger coaches and a locomotive with a torch for a headlight. From the jail and along Pearl Street to the train armed men stood guard to prevent any alarm being given to the citizens. At the depot, foot of State Street, the night engineer, Richard Johnson, and conductor, A. W. Hamline, were placed under guard and kept in the office while the mob were at work. When they returned Johnson was called out and told to start up. Hamline came to the door, but was told to remain where he was.

The train left here about four o'clock, and when near the State Prison, as we learn from one of the attaches of the road, it was stopped and the men got off, telling the engineer to return to the city at once.

As soon as the train left, Mr. Perrette went in search of a physician to dress the sheriff's wound, but before he reached the jail the alarm had been sounded and quite a crowd had collected. . . .

It is estimated that there were from seventy-five to a hundred men in the party, but who they are is as yet unknown. They came well armed and equipped for their work, and executed it in less time than a person would imagine it could be done, as they were not over twenty minutes at the jail. They had five manila ropes each about eight or ten feet long, with hangman's noose already to slip over the heads of their victims. One of these ropes was left behind, and it is supposed they intended to hang Clark, who is here on a change of venue from Washington County, for the murder of George Telle, but they concluded not to do so, fearing to remain longer, lest the alarm might be given. . . .

It is understood that Reno and Anderson intended to apply before Judge Bicknell for a writ of *habeas corpus*, saying they could show that they were not concerned in the Marshfield robbery. The so-called Vigilantes probably got wind of this, and hence the terrible tragedy of this morning.

Mrs. Anderson stated to our reporter that Charles Anderson was in bed with her, his wife, at their residence in Windsor, Canada, on the night of the Express robbery at Marshfield. She also states that Frank Reno was boarding at her house, and was there that night. Mrs. S. V. Reno, wife of Frank Reno, asserts that Wm. Reno was at the Rader House in Seymour on the night of the robbery, and that Simeon was at Rockford. The party were no doubt bad men, and had committed crimes against the law, but they were at east entitled to a fair trial.

It may be remembered that Charles Anderson and Frank Reno had their residence at Windsor, Canada. Soon after the Marshfield Express robbery, an application was made to the Canadian authorities for their surrender under the extradition treaty, on a charge of being implicated in the robbery. A lengthy examination ensued, and a great many witnesses were examined. One witness swore that he recognized the two men as being concerned in the robbery, but by others they proved that they were at Windsor on the night of the robbery.

The counsel for the prisoners urged that in a case of so much doubt it would be little less than murder to deliver them up, inasmuch as the mob which had already hung six men, stood ready to hang Reno and Anderson, should they be delivered up. This seemed to have weight with the magistrate, when the Adams Express Company pledged themselves, and we have heard gave bond, that they should have a fair and impartial trial. Upon a representation of the facts to our Government at Washington, Secretary Seward also gave a solemn pledge that the men should have a fair trial, and if found innocent of this charge they should be returned by the United States to their residence in Canada. . . .

It is but just to Sheriff Fullenlove to say that he did his duty in this most trying crisis of his life fully, manfully, nobly. Though threatened with instant death, and actually shot in the arm, and stunned by a blow over the eye, he refused to deliver up to the mob the keys to the jail.

Throughout the day which followed the lynching, hundreds of townspeople trouped by the county jail to take a final look at the four dead men lying in their crude coffins.

Nearly twenty years later the gates of Missouri State Prison swung open and John Reno—whose criminal career had begun at the age of eleven and had spawned tragedy for his brothers—rode out to freedom. He was a greying man, in fairly good health, but a lonely man with nothing but his tortured conscience to keep him company. None of his family was left to greet him, and nobody knows what became of him.

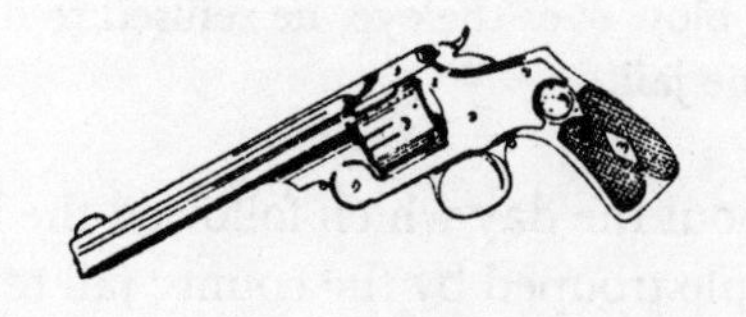

5 Sam Bass

On July 21, 1878, the streets of Round Rock, Texas, were heavy with oppressive heat and thick with strangers, who were crowding the hotels, sleeping in halls and lobbies, or camping out at the edge of town. In the first hours of daylight they were walking the dusty streets and staring curiously at the mute jail-house walls—for they were waiting for a man to die.

A tired Negro snapped the strings of a guitar and sang:

> 'Sam Bass was born in Indiana,
> It was his native home.
> When at the age of seventeen
> Young Sam Bass began to roam.
> He first came down to Texas,
> A teamster for to be,
> A kinder-hearted fellow
> You hardly ever see.'

Thus Sam Bass was a Texas legend even before he was dead. Sentimentalists called him 'noble desperado'; the Press published poetry on his courage and dash and generosity. In the jail-house a Texas Ranger's bullet was taking its toll. Sam Bass was dying of a gunshot wound.

Major John B. Jones of the Texas Rangers leaned over his cot. At times Sam would talk guardedly to Dr. Cochran or Major Jones, giving information, but never anything to incriminate an ally. When asked a point-blank question he would always give the same reply:

'It's agin my profession to blow on my pals. If a man knows anything important he oughta die with it in him.'

Although Bass in his dying hours steadfastly held back all damaging information about his pals, he himself had been betrayed by one of his own men. Before that July day was over Sam Bass was dead, and Jim Murphy, train robber and gunman, emerged from a fabulous cloak-and-dagger crime story as the most famous squealer in the history of Texas.

Sam Bass was a product of Indiana, born near Mitchell, in Lawrence County, on July 21, 1851. He died twenty-seven years later to the day. An orphan, Sam was brought up on the prosperous farm of an uncle, whose shelter he left at eighteen, with a love of horses that drove him to Denton County, Texas.

Stoop-shouldered, around five feet eight and with the appearance of a whipped pup, he was a hard worker as a teamster. He showed no sign in his general attitude of any criminal tendencies. In disputes with other people he resorted to the courts for settlement. But it was one minor brush with the law that snowballed and developed a two-fisted life of crime for the young man from Indiana. Riding into Denton with Henry Underwood one hot summer afternoon in 1875, Bass dropped a large melon and a group of young Negroes laughed at the spectacle. Bass and Underwood leaped off their horses and began to stone the boys, who complained to the sheriff. He placed the men under arrest and, outraged, they galloped out of town with the sheriff firing after them.

Sheriff Gerren swore out a warrant against them and sent a posse in vain pursuit. It may betray a weak character in Bass to have plunged bitterly into a wild tear that led to robbery and bloodshed, but this minor conflict was the trigger to Bass's lawless career.

Underwood, a heavy drinker and a trouble-maker by nature, had no qualms about going the wrong way with Bass. It has been said that in the four years that followed he was actually the brains of the Bass gang, and this is probable, since Bass, shrewd as he was, did not have the ability to plan some of the more intricate holdups.

Underwood, also a native of Indiana, born in 1846, had already been a member of the infamous Jennison's Jayhawkers of Kansas, guerrillas who fought against Quantrill's men. After Lee's surrender Underwood married a fine woman, and for a few years led a calm, sociable life. Once he journeyed to Texas, however, his guerrilla traits returned, and he became a loud-mouth and a tough who couldn't keep out of trouble.

After he and Sam Bass had shaken off the posse at a tangled ravine called Hickory Bottom, Underwood went to South-west Texas, posing as a cattle-buyer, and Sam went to San Antonio, where he met Joel (Joe) Collins, a daredevil who came from a fine San Antonio family and held a good job. They tried a couple of petty robberies, but decided burglary was not worth the effort. Using Collins's savings as a down payment, they purchased a herd of cattle and set out for Kansas cattle centres. The herd earned them a fair profit, but they went on a drunken binge and woke up one morning penniless.

They had just met Jack Davis, an ex-cowhand who was talking about Deadwood, South Dakota.

'Wide open and ready to be picked,' he told them.

The three men decided to give the raw, rip-roaring young town a try. Bass recruited three desperadoes, Bill Heffridge, Tom Nixon, and Jim Berry, to fill out the band. Jack Davis was ready to get into anything, since Deadwood was a city of saloons and women—costly for a man who liked that sort of thing. Bass outlined an idea to take on the Deadwood Stage Line, and during the summer of 1877 the gang preyed on the stagecoaches. But by summer's end they were discouraged.

'Hell!' Collins said bitterly. 'We ain't taken enough to make it worth the effort.' So he outlined a new plan.

Collins kept an eagle eye on the stageline, and an ear to the ground. Towards the last of August the word was whispered around.

'You heard? Big load comin' in from the mines. Dust and money. Deadwood stage is really gonna be loaded down next run.'

'This is it,' Collins told Bass. 'This one haul will be enough.'

Collins had the date and trail lined up. The stage was leaving the rough, gold-ripped hills early in the morning to bring the load into Deadwood. The gang picked their spot, a ravine thick with tangled brush and trees. Collins and Heffridge each took positions to one side, while the other four stretched out along the trail. The first two represented what was to be the initial attack. If they ran into serious trouble Bass and the remainder of the gang could back them up.

About 11 a.m. the coach came rocking along the wilderness trail. Inside four guards rode with shotguns, outside the rider whipped his frothy horses towards Deadwood. Collins and Heffridge spurred their horses on to the trail, guns cocked and ready. But the driver did the unexpected. Instead of hauling up at the sight of the two masked gunmen, he lashed out at Collins with his bullwhip.

'Hi—y-i-i-i!' the driver bellowed, and the horses plunged ahead down the trail in billowing dust.

Collins and Heffridge blasted, and the quiet sunny morning erupted with the sound of racking gunfire. The driver stiffened, never got his gun out. His body bounced from the seat and hung on the edge of the stage. The inside of the coach burst alive. Guns blazed as the guards cut loose at the robbers. Bass and his section plunged out of the thickets, guns roaring. Dust spat around them and the stage clattered past, the panicked horses dashing down the trail, the coach crashing behind it, spitting bullets.

Down through the ravine and across the flat the horses ran, the coach tearing behind them, over rocks, ditches, ripping up stumps, the guards tossed like rag dolls inside, the bandits rushing along behind, their bullets smacking into the stage. As the paper-box saloon town loomed ahead, Bass and his men were forced to pull leather and abandon the chase.

News of the death of the stage-driver spread, and word got around that Collins had been seen. Other men remembered he had asked questions about the stagecoach and its lucrative load. However, before the bandits could be taken into custody they split up. Joel Collins and Heffridge went together, Nixon and Berry paired off, and Bass and Jack Davis hit the trail in another direction. By separating for the time being they eluded the posse that was organized in Deadwood, but a month later the six were once more together at Collins's hideaway in the Dakota Badlands.

'We've got to leave the territory,' Berry suggested. 'There's a deputy behind every rock in Dakota. We stay around and sure's hell we'll hang.'

Collins said: 'The Union Pacific runs through Ogallala, Nebraska. On our way back south we can pick it off.'

Collins had an information pipeline into Ogallala through his common-law wife. The men split up again, with Collins's mistress acting as a central intelligence clearing-post. Bass and Davis were camped some miles away when a messenger summoned them, warning them to ride around Duck Creek, which was said to be swarming with soldiers.

The band assembled outside Deadwood and rode towards Nebraska. It took nearly a week of hard travel to get to Ogallala and, once there, they changed plans again.

'Too many people,' Collins said. 'And I don't like the lay of the land. We'll pick another spot.'

Big Springs Station, several miles west of Ogallala, afforded them a better position. They secreted themselves around the water-station at Big Springs on September 18, 1877—and before the day ended their escapade at Big Springs was to resound to the four corners of the U.S.A.

The entire holdup took ten minutes, and the loot ran higher than sixty thousand dollars. Thus began a series of adroit train robberies that brought the Pinkertons in with railroad law agencies and Government forces in a fabulous manhunt. Underwood, innocent of any part in this train robbery, was arrested and jailed as Tom Nixon. Joel Collins and Bill Heffridge were ambushed on the Kansas prairie and cut down shooting by a sheriff, some railroad detectives, and ten U.S. cavalrymen. Berry was shot trying to escape from his own house in Missouri by the sheriff of the town. And Bass, recruiting new men as he went—a tinker named Frank Jackson joined him early, and was his last ally—always returned in his circular elusions to Denton, where he began his disastrous career.

As the weeks rolled by, the Bass band grew more and more daring in its work, looting stagecoaches and the Texas railroads in a wide sweep that always brought them back to Denton County. Bass recruited a wanderer named Sebe Barnes and then a wanted killer called Tom Spotswood, and, with the same basic procedure learned from the Renos, carried on his brazen looting of the Texas trains.

Bass had by now become the object of a Statewide manhunt, with large rewards posted for his capture. Sheriff Egan of Denton sent to the Bass camp spies who successfully set traps for the outlaws by giving Bass false information. But each time Egan set his ambush Texas Rangers happened to be seen locally by one of the outlaws.

Egan became an object of criticism for failing to catch the local badmen. Newspapers throughout Texas were blaming Denton people for the crime wave, and the citizens in turn focused their anger on the local law. Some even hinted that Egan must be in league with the robbers. His unfortunate deputies were also criticized.

In the latter part of March, Deputy-Sheriff Wetsel suggested that he gain entrance to the Bass hideout on some ruse and then devise a plan by which the outlaw chieftain could be captured. He rode out to the Murphy ranch and told Bass's friend that he had information for Bass. Murphy was suspicious at first, but decided it would do no harm to take Wetsel into the stronghold. He led Wetsel down through the twisted overgrowth to the creek bottom where Bass, Barnes, and Jackson were in hiding. Bass was civil enough to Wetsel, but was careful not to mention any of the robberies. Actually, the law had nothing but suspicion against him.

'Let's have a few games of poker,' Bass suggested. After a few hands, Bass jumped up, his hand on his gun-butt.

Two men rode into the camp. One was Billy Scott and the other Billy Collins.

'We're with a couple of fellows who want to see you,' Collins said. 'One of 'em's Arkansas Johnson and the other one's Hank Underwood.'

'Underwood!' Bass said. 'I'll be damned.'

They summoned the Nebraska fugitive, and he and his new partner rode into camp.

For the moment Wetsel was forgotten. At the time he had in his pocket a warrant for Underwood's arrest on a charge of escaping from the Nebraska jail. When the reunion had simmered down, Wetsel told Underwood he was going to take him in.

'No, you ain't,' Bass said sternly.

Wetsel looked from one bandit face to the next and slid the warrant back into his pocket.

During the time Wetsel was there he didn't realize that an informer was in the camp. Billy Scott at this time was working under orders from Major Jones of the Texas Rangers. He did not know of Wetsel's plan, and Wetsel wasn't aware of Scott's role in the drama.

Bass and his men moved away from their camp to prevent a possible ambush by Wetsel's friends. Bass was ready to try another holdup, but his men weren't so enthusiastic. Underwood wanted to visit his family, which he hadn't seen for months. Barnes was ill, and Frank Jackson cried off. Actually Jackson had been trying to quit the gang, but Bass had too strong a hold on him. Bass and Johnson headed for Dallas County to stage a robbery by themselves.

'We can pick up a couple of boys on the way,' Bass said.

On April 5, 1878, Bass, Johnson, and two new recruits

arrived at Eagle Ford, Texas. Throughout the day they studied the station and the country around. The next day they slept and then just before midnight concealed themselves under the station platform to await the arrival of the train. As the train pulled in they masked their faces and rushed out, quickly commandeering the engine. Bass had the fireman and engine-driver taken to the station and assigned one man to guard them and the station agent. Bass jumped back aboard the train and shattered the express car door. The messenger never fired a shot. He stood rooted in his tracks as two men burst into the car.

'Open the box!' Bass ordered.

The messenger complied quickly. The thieves were disappointed in their haul, since only a small amount of cash and some registered mail were inside. Not a shot had been fired.

'It went off like clockwork,' Bass said later.

His two recruits, whose identity was never learned, were not impressed with the theft since the loot was so small. They quickly retired, so Bass and Johnson rode back to the brush.

The Government was now demanding action from law-enforcement officers, and Denton County was swarming with police, including the Texas Rangers. Yet Sam Bass was harder to catch than a greased owl. He seemed to know the actions of the law officers before they were made, since he had many friends willing to serve him. The police realized that to ride into the wilds of his hiding-place was to ask for death.

Billy Collins had become an important member of the band. He was Joel's brother, and anxious to avenge his brother's death at Buffalo Station. Bass decided to use him on the next holdup as a contact man.

'The next job is the train at Mesquite. Billy, you go on down there and look over the lay of the land.'

Collins lived near Mesquite, and the gang forgathered there.

The robbery was set for Tuesday, April 9, 1878, but the train was late arriving at the station, and the outlaws thought they had missed it, so they returned to Collins's home to await the train the following day. On Wednesday, the tenth, the bandits rode into Mesquite separately and concealed themselves behind the depot. Nearby, a group of convicts were working on a construction gang guarded by several men with double-barrelled shotguns. They were to add to the confusion.

From accounts, the Mesquite robbery was not so well planned as the preceding holdups. As the train rolled into the station, the masked bandits jumped out on the platform.

'Hold up your hands,' one of them cried to the conductor, Captain J. Alvord. 'This is a robbery.'

Alvord whirled and ran back up into the car after a larger revolver, since he was carrying only a derringer which would be of no use in a gunfight. One of the bandits snapped a shot at him as he disappeared back into the car. Alvord grabbed a six-gun, smashed a window, and blasted back. Up front, the brave engine-driver threw off the brake and jammed the throttle.

The train began to roll out of the station. One of the bandits leaped on the passenger coach and slipped by the door. Alvord fired at him. The outlaw stepped into the doorway and fired back. Alvord twisted as a bullet ripped through his arm and rolled through the door at the other end of the coach, bullets tearing through the floor behind him. He fired back at the bandit, but his arm was bleeding so badly that he hastened into the sleeping-coach and yanked a sheet off one of the berths to bind the wound.

Meanwhile, another one of the bandits rode alongside the engine and jumped into it from his horse. He ordered the driver to haul in the brakes.

On the platform, one of the passengers, D. J. Healy of Dallas, a friend of the station-master, had been held up as he stepped off the train. As his guard turned to help stop the train, Healy hurriedly secreted his money in his shoe. Then he darted off behind the station. The outlaw spotted him and fired several times. Healy rushed down the tracks to the construction gang.

'A holdup!' he yelled. 'Back at the station. They're holding up the train!'

Then he ducked under the construction car. The guards, however, could not leave the convicts. They stood helplessly by while the melodrama was played out.

The train had now been hauled to a stop, and the station-agent was held at bay with a cocked revolver. A young woman in the station turned screaming as she saw the masked gunman step into the station. Instead of throwing up her hands as ordered, she ran into the rest-room and bolted the door.

Sam Bass and two of his men swung up to the express car and ordered the messenger to open up. Curly, the messenger, refused to unlatch the door.

'If that's your answer,' Bass bellowed, 'we'll set the car afire. You'll fry in there!'

Bass poured a can of oil across the front of the door and yelled: 'The door's oiled, man. Open it or we touch her off.'

Back down the tracks Alvord's gun boomed again. By now other guns were roaring and the air was rancid with smoke.

The messenger jerked open the door and stepped back into the car, hands over his head. Bass smashed the safe open and gasped in utter dismay. It contained only a hundred and fifty dollars.

'Let's get outa here,' he snapped.

The three men abandoned the car, and the bandits began to flee. More shots rang out. Underwood and Sebe Barnes both winced as bullets ripped through their arms. The bandit gang, including a wounded man named Pipes, whipped their horses and rode off. As they dashed past the construction gang, the guards opened fire with their shotguns, but none took effect. Underwood left the gang after his wound was bound and he went into hiding. Barnes and Pipes found refuge in Collins's home.

The name of Sam Bass had by now become a household symbol of terror from Galveston to the Panhandle. State police officers and auxiliary county officers were dispatched to

Denton County with orders to get Bass dead or alive. Major Jones left from Dallas with a group of Texas Rangers under command of Lieutenant June Peak, to begin a vigorous scouring of the entire county. Jones had made rendezvous with Billy Scott, who had supplied pertinent facts relating to the robberies, such as the identities of the robbers and their hiding-places.

Jones first concentrated on Pipes and a recruit named Herndon who, according to Scott, were at the home of Henry Collins, another brother of the late Joel.

Scott went to the Collins's house and found Pipes there. When he failed to return that night, Jones surrounded the place and rushed in, arresting Scott, Pipes, and Collins. Herndon was arrested the same day at the Jackson ranch, several miles away.

Scott and Collins were released, and Pipes and Herndon were whisked away to Tyler for trial in the dead of night. William Collins was called to Tyler as a witness, but when he arrived he found that he had been tricked. He was served a warrant implicating him in the robberies.

After these arrests, Billy Scott decided to pay another visit to the Bass camp and try to smoke out the others, so that he could collect the large rewards posted on every tree and in front of every marshal's office in the State. He fired Bass's imagination when he suggested robbing the Gaston and Exchange Bank in Dallas. Partial plans were made, and he returned to report the plot to Jones. But Henry Collins, innocent yet implicated in the Mesquite robbery, had fled when he was warned that a warrant had once again been issued against him, and he had also been warned that Scott was a spy. Collins raced to the Bass camp and told them to kill Scott the minute he returned. Major Jones, however, was beginning to worry about Scott's constant risks and forbade him to return to the Bass stronghold. This was a lucky break for Scott.

Rangers now invaded the Hickory Branch hideout, and Bass and his men were forced to run. They kept on the move, and Bass displayed an amazing knack for keeping his men out of reach. Sheriff Everheart of Grayson County entered the northern part of Denton County, while Sheriff Egan patrolled the rest of the county. For weeks Bass kept them on the run, moving at night, circling the lawmen and defacing his tracks so that he couldn't be trailed.

It was not until April 29, a Sunday, that the law finally made contact. Bass had stopped for a breather at Murphy's ranch, and one of the lookouts spotted Everheart heading for Cove Hollow.

'I'm tired o' runnin',' Bass said. 'We know the Hollow better 'n that bunch. Let's go give 'em a little hell.'

The outlaws rode to Cove Hollow, which was a deep canyon, and spread out among the rocks and bushes, waiting for the law. Everheart came over the opposite ridge, smart enough to keep out of the canyon bottom and thus avoid being cut down from above. The canyon erupted with gunfire. The law on one side of the canyon and Bass and his gang on the other blasted away at each other. With Everheart was an expert marksman. He crawled to the edge of the canyon rim, spotted Bass, and made him a special target. His first shot ripped through the stock of Bass's rifle. The second smacked into his cartridge belt, knocking his wind out.

'The hell with this!' Bass bellowed. 'Let's get outa here.'

Bass was on the run again, but the law officers spurred hard after him. That evening Deputy-Sheriff Wetsel was patrolling the road near Bolivar with Constable McGintie. About ten miles north of Denton they saw the fleeing outlaws and pursued them until dark. The next morning they and their men were joined by Captain Whitehead. They began to track the bandits on foot through a field behind Whitehead's Farm, which ended at Clear Creek Bottom. As they stepped over the bank of the creek they saw Bass and his gang pulling out through the brush. Wetsel got his horse and started through the swamps and brush after them, while McGintie and Whitehead returned to the farm for more horses. Bass rode rapidly to a new camp at Hard Carter's ranch, four miles south-east of Denton. McGintie, Wetsel, and Whitehead tracked them there and then hid out nearby, sending word to Sheriff Egan.

Egan made rendezvous with Wetsel and surrounded the Carter ranch, while the deputy slipped through the brush to reconnoitre and discovered that the bandits were bedded down several hundred yards from the Carter house. Sneaking back to the house, he started questioning Carter.

Then Bass walked in!

Wetsel dived for cover, and Bass pulled out his gun, yelling to his gang to run for it. The two men opened fire on each other, and bullets ripped through the Carter house. Peeling shots off with his thumb, Bass slipped through a window and jumped on his horse. The rest of the band met him as he rode away, and they charged past the posse surrounding the house, low in the saddle, guns roaring.

Both sides were beginning to weary. Horses were tired. The men had been days without bathing or proper rest. They were bedraggled, bearded, and falling asleep in the saddle. But the chase continued.

On Wednesday morning, May 1, Lieutenant Peak rode up on Bass as he was preparing breakfast in a wooded stretch four miles outside Denton. The bandits barely had time to escape. Peak and his men caught one of their horses and found breakfast still simmering over the fire. He divided his command and scoured the entire countryside. Four days later he gave up the search.

Bass had eluded one of the most sprawling, dedicated dragnets in police history. He was still on the loose.

Sheriff Everheart reported that he did not know where Bass and his men were. It seemed that, since the gang had evaded the lawmen concentrated in Denton, Wise, and Grayson Counties, they must have headed for Mexico or for Indian Territory. Everheart declared that, since the whole countryside was alive with scouting parties trying to capture the outlaws for the sake of the reward, his efforts were greatly impeded, and he believed there were several bands pretending to hunt Bass who were actually his accomplices, keeping him posted on the lawmen.

Excitement over the Bass chase was temporarily checked while the big news was the trial of Herndon and Pipes at Tyler. But on May 18 the following telegram from Fort Griffin revived interest:

Sam Bass with five of his men is surrounded on Big Caddo Creek by Berry Meadows, sheriff of Stephens County. Meadows was reinforced by ten men from Palo Pinto last night at two o'clock. He expected to make the attack by daylight this morning. Some fighting was done yesterday and the day before. No damage done on our side. It was not known whether any outlaws were hurt.

The attempt at the capture was described by the *Fort Worth Democrat*:

Deputy-Sheriff Freeman was informed last week by a woman of the neighbourhood, near Caddo Creek, that parties answering to the description of the train robbers were there. He, with one Ranger, and Messrs. Amis and Paschell of this town, went into that section to ascertain something more definite, and learned that Bass, Underwood, Jackson, Barnes, and two others, supposed to be Welch and Collins, had been camped there in the mountains for upwards of two weeks. A brother-in-law of Jackson, and several other kin and friends are living near Caddo Creek, and had furnished them with supplies. They are reported to be flush with twenty-dollar gold pieces, and from events developed more recently, they are found to have numerous friends in that vicinity. Having gathered the desired information, the Ranger reported to his camp in Shackelford County, and the balance repaired to Breckenridge, where Sheriff Meadows and Deputies Freeman and Hood selected several picked men, and on Sunday started for the scene of action. At midnight they sent back for reinforcements, and twenty old shotguns were collected together and the same number of volunteers. Before all of these new recruits arrived, the sheriff's posse came upon the gang near the store, thirteen miles east of here, on the

Palo Pinto road, and an engagement ensued, in which about forty shots were fired by each party, and at one time three of the party dismounted and fought from behind trees. It is thought one of their horses was wounded. They afterwards chased the robbers about two miles into the mountains. As the gang was so much better armed than the sheriff's party, and were acquainted with the locality of the mountain defiles, they then had little to fear. On Monday night they camped among the trees and thickets near Taylor's store, and the sheriff's party on the prairie one-third mile distant.

Tuesday morning, May 26, the Sheriff and his posse were gladdened by the arrival of the gallant Rangers from Shackelford County, nineteen in number, armed to the teeth, and their force had also been increased by Deputy-Sheriff Owen and eight picked men from Palo Pinto town. The Rangers were under the command of Lieut. Campbell and Sergeant Jack Smith, and the Breckenridge party of fearless Deputy-Sheriff Freeman. Sergeant Smith, of the Rangers, stated that if they could find them, they would capture the robbers dead or alive, if they lost half their men in the attempt. On Tuesday they followed their trail through mountains, gaps, and defiles, and among the hills and valleys in their winding course, but up to twelve o'clock last night had not overtaken them, though the gang had come back to near the starting-point. At McClasen's store, four miles further east, they purchased eight dollars' worth of provisions, and left word for the pursuers that they would stand their ground and give them a desperate fight, and that they did not propose to be bulldozed, all of which is supposed to be a blind, and that they in reality were preparing to strike out for parts unknown. It was ascertained that they had been trying to swap one of their horses. They are said to be well mounted and each armed with a Winchester rifle and a pair of six-shooters. Before the arrival of the Rangers, the Sheriff had summoned four or five citizens in that neighbourhood to secure arms and join his posse.

The Bass gang passed the same party soon after, before they had obtained arms, marched them down to the store and treated to bottle beer. It is said that parties in that vicinity have carried the Bass gang baskets of provisions and kept them informed of the movement of their pursuers. One of the gang, it is reported, is suffering from a wound received in Denton County. One of them remarked to some person at the store that they were no petty thieves, that they interfered with no private citizen, but, holding out a handful of twenty-dollar gold pieces, said, 'That is what the Sheriff and his posse want.'

But once again the elusive Bass foiled the law. Efforts to surround the gang proved unavailing, and a few days later, on May 31, the sheriff telegraphed from Breckenridge that his posse and the Rangers had given up the chase and they had left Bass commanding the situation in the rugged mountains fifteen miles east of the place.

During the Breckenridge chase, a grocer named Nance informed a local deputy-sheriff that Bass had bought provisions at his store and he understood the bandits were headed for Taylor's store, some miles away. The officer gathered four local farmers, armed them with shotguns, and rode a few miles. They spotted the Bass crew, riding leisurely as though without a care in the world.

The deputy-sheriff instructed the four farmers to take to the timber at both sides of the road and head off the gang. In the meantime he remained behind the group to prevent them from retreating. The farmers rode through the trees to a spot ahead of the outlaws and dismounted.

As the outlaw chieftain drew abreast of the four men, one of them stood up and ordered sternly: 'All right! Drop your guns and surrender. You're under arrest.'

The words were no sooner out of his mouth than a blood-curdling scream came out of the woods behind them. The farmers froze in their tracks and almost ran into each other in frightened disorder. Bass and his outlaws struck into the woods and quickly disarmed the four would-be heroes. The deputy-sheriff wheeled in his tracks and fled for his life.

Hank Underwood came out of the forest with a smile on his face. While acting as scout for the robbers, he had been following the farmers.

Instead of harming the four lawmen, Bass and his gang

took them to Taylor's store, and in less than an hour they were all roaring drunk. When the men woke up next morning, their heads pounding with hangovers, the gang was gone. They had left behind a note:

'Don't try any more tricks on Sam Bass.'

Early one June morning Bass and his men dashed through the streets of Denton and pulled up in front of Charlie McDonald's stable.

'Where's that horse Egan took from me back in May?' Bass demanded.

McDonald's eyes bulged, and he stammered through his beard. Then, regaining control of himself, he stoutly refused to say anything and was whacked across the side of the head.

Bass turned to a new recruit named Carter, who was reputed to be a cattle thief. 'Go back in the barn and get us three horses,' he said.

Carter rode through the barn, rounded up three animals, and came back.

During that time a man armed with a double-barrelled shotgun lay gulping in amazement in the hayloft. He didn't fire a shot. With their horses in tow, the gang started out of town, but they made one stop—in front of Sheriff Egan's house.

'Hey, Sheriff,' Bass yelled. 'Get outa bed. The whole country's full of thieves.'

Egan leaped out of bed and went hopping to the window, his leg shoved into his trousers. The town seemed to come alive with people rushing through the streets.

'Sam Bass is back!' they yelled.

The chase began at once. Captain Withers from nearby Elizabeth rode into town. He had been tracking the bandit crew since the day before, when someone had spotted them near his town. Withers immediately took up the pursuit and overtook the gang about six miles south of Denton at a place called Pilot Knob.

Bass and his men dismounted and opened fire as Withers's

crew rode into sight. George Smith, marshal of Denton, was blown out of the saddle and lay in the dust with bullets spitting around him. Withers turned to one of his men and ordered him back to Denton for reinforcements, but Bass saw him jump on his horse and, leaping on his own mount, he cut through the brush and intercepted the rider before he got to town.

'Hold it!' he ordered, gun cocked.

The rider pulled up, eyes wide with fear.

'Get off the horse, son, and stop botherin' us,' Bass said.

The amazed rider stood in the road and watched Bass ride off leading his horse.

Egan meanwhile was racing to the scene. He staked out his men to set up a crossfire, but one of the deputies shot the hapless Wetsel through a leg by accident. The rest of the posse, now numbering fifty men, continued to pursue Bass.

During the next two days the chase continued over rocky terrain, through woods, across creeks, and into swamps. Several times there were brief skirmishes, but nobody was hurt. On June 10 the bandits broke into the open prairie, and Everheart and his posse raced across the wastes after them. The bandits and lawmen exchanged shot after shot in the running gun battle, but they were out of range of each other. Finally the gang wheeled into the mountains and disappeared up a narrow draw.

The lawmen sat exhausted in their saddles, soaked through with sweat.

'The hell with it!' Egan said disgustedly.

The posse turned back towards Denton.

Egan's temper would have been much improved had he known of the events to come, for Lieutenant Peak and the Texas Rangers scored the first real damage to the Bass outlaws. Six days after the prairie gun battle, Peak and his command picked up the trail of the gang along Salt Creek, near Cottondale. Peak's Rangers beat through the dense bush most of the day, then in the afternoon they suddenly walked up on the whole bunch lounging under a tree on the bank of the creek, their horses a few yards away.

The Rangers plunged into the stream, guns firing. The battle was the bitterest fought in the entire pursuit. The woods were torn with lead.

Sergeant Jack Floyd, a crack shot, spotted Bass and Arkansas Johnson untying the horses. He dropped to one knee and fired a single shot. Arkansas Johnson, one of Sam's closest friends, whirled away from his horse and fell into the bushes, dead.

Bass blasted back angrily. His men dashed to their horses and then saddled up one at a time while the others kept things hot. But in the blistering gun battle only Underwood, Collins, and Carter escaped on horseback. The rest of the men took to the brush, with the Rangers fighting the dense undergrowth. Underwood crashed out of the hot spot, for he had had enough. It was the last time Bass ever saw him.

As they rushed through the jungle, Jackson turned.

'Where's Arkansas?' he asked.

'Took one right in the head,' Bass said. 'He's gone.'

The death of Johnson hit Bass hard, for he had been the boldest of the freebooters, quick to size up a situation or an enemy. It had been Johnson who had taken one look at Billy Scott and warned that he was a spy.

'I should have taken his word and killed Scott the first time he said anything,' Bass said later.

Amazingly enough, Bass actually eluded the Texas Rangers on foot in the dense Salt Creek tangles. Later, Sam said he lay out in the bushes while the Rangers passed ten feet in front of him. After they broke out of the brush, the remainder of the outlaws easily found assistance from the local farmers. With fresh horses they rode off, beating the law once more.

The Salt Creek fight virtually ended the campaign against Bass. In seven weeks none of the outlaws had been captured and only one was dead, so the law gave up.

Jim Murphy had of course been in close alliance with the

Bass crew when they had lived in Hickory Bottom and in Cove Hollow, both of which were near his ranch. Both Murphy and his father, Henderson Murphy, had been arrested for harbouring the outlaws and had been among the prisoners taken to Tyler. Murphy had at first planned to escape if possible and join Bass, but now things looked different to him.

Perhaps it was Scott's testimony which led Murphy to offer to betray Bass in exchange for freedom. On July 26 he made the following proposal to the Texas Rangers at Austin:

I, J. W. Murphy, was arrested May 1, 1878, by Sheriff Everheart, of Grayson County, for harbouring Sam Bass. I was innocent of the charge, and told Everheart so. I asked him why he did not tell me long ago that he wanted Sam Bass. He gave me no answer of any satisfaction, but pushed me off from my family and put me in jail at Sherman. Walter Johnson took me from the Sherman jail and put me in jail in Tyler. On the way to the jail at Tyler I hinted the plan for capturing Sam Bass to Taylor and he said he would send Johnson to see me soon. Johnson came to see me after I had given bond. I told him that I could plan a job to capture Sam Bass if I was footloose. Johnson told me that he would see me again soon. So he went off and came back with June Peak, and we talked the matter over. June says, 'I will go and see Major Jones.' The Major came and talked with me about the plan for the capture of Bass. At this time I made a contract with Major Jones as to what he would do for me and my father if I would catch Sam Bass. He said if I would lay the plan for the capture of Sam Bass, that he would have my case and my father's dismissed and that he would see that I should have my part of the reward and his part too. He said that he did not want any of the reward, and that I should have what was right. I worked this plan under three men, Jones, Peak, and Johnson. Nobody else was to know anything about it. They were the men I relied on. After a short time Sheriff Everheart worked into the secret through Johnson. The first time that Everheart came to me I gave him no satisfaction. The second time he came a man by the name of Taylor was with him. Taylor told me that whatever Everheart told me would be all right with Johnson, and I let him into the secret against my own will.

The following is the text of the agreement entered into with the United States Attorney, Andrew J. Evans:

Whereas, James Murphy stands indicted as an accessory in robbing the United States mail, in several cases now pending in the United States District Court at Tyler, and whereas, I believe public justice will be best subserved, hereby, I, Andrew J. Evans, United States Attorney for the Western District of Texas, bind the United States as follows:

1st. If the said Murphy should leave Tyler I will protect him and his bondsman at this term of the court.

2nd. If the said Murphy shall be instrumental in securing the arrest and delivery to the United States Marshal of the Western District of Texas, of all or any one of the following principals, in their order (Bass, Jackson, Underwood, Barnes, and Johnson), in said indictments, then all prosecutions are to be dismissed as to said Murphy, growing out of his acts as accessory to the said principals; to be done upon certificate of Major John B. Jones.

3rd. In case the said Murphy shall use all reasonable and possible means in his power to capture the said Bass and his above-named associates, and if Major John B. Jones will certify to such facts to the United States Attorney, then the said Murphy is to have the relief named in section 2nd above, although he may be unsuccessful.

(Signed) A. J. Evans
U. S. Attorney

May 21st, 1878.

In order to convince Murphy of his sincerity and his power to keep his bargain, Major Jones's first act was to dismiss the charges against Murphy's father and to obtain his release. With instructions to carry out his part of the agreement faithfully, Murphy was then also allowed to go free. It was published in the newspapers that he had jumped his bond and had fled that part of the State.

Jones also kept Lieutenant Peak's command at Dallas so that Murphy would know where they were at all times and could make his plans accordingly. Upon receiving word from

Murphy, Peak was to proceed to his assistance with his entire command. With the public and the Press clamouring for the arrest of Sam Bass and his men, Jones was inviting criticism by keeping the Peak command tied up in Dallas.

On May 21, when Murphy was released from Tyler, he returned immediately to his home on the Denton-Cooke county line. His plan was to wait for Bass to seek him out.

On June 6 Bass returned to Denton County and he went straight to the Murphy ranch.

Murphy rushed out of the ranch to greet him. Like Judas, he acted overjoyed at seeing the bandit chieftain again and greeted him with questions. Murphy fed the men and then sent them off to the Cove Hollow hideout. Since he now knew that Sheriff Everheart was also in on the secret plan, he decided to lure the group to the ranch-house at an appointed time and betray them to the Denton County lawman. The trap was set, but never sprung, because for some reason Everheart failed to show up at the meeting.

When the band got ready to leave, Murphy decided to join them, since his bid for freedom depended upon his keeping these men under his thumb all the time, so he selected a good horse and several weapons and rode off with the outlaws. They headed for Bolivar and from there went to Wise County, where the Salt Creek battle had occurred. Then, with stolen horses, Bass and his remaining party headed back to Denton County.

Camped in a church the outlaw band was joined also by Henry Collins and a stranger. Collins wasted little time giving Bass his news.

'Word's got around the Ranger station at Fort Worth,' Collins said, 'that Murphy's a traitor in your camp. They say he's keeping the Rangers posted every time you move your little finger.'

Murphy's skin turned cold. Bass, Jackson, Barnes, and Collins, desperate and running for their lives, faced him.

'Well, what about that?' Bass said, his hand on his gun.

'It's a damned lie!' Murphy squeaked.

'You better make it good, Jim,' Bass said, drawing his gun and thumbing back the hammer; ' 'cause if it ain't good you ain't gonna walk out of this church.'

'It was just a trick on my part,' Murphy said. 'I had to get away from them damn peace officers in Dallas, some way.'

'I think he's okay,' Jackson interceded. 'I've knowed Jim since we was boys together. He ain't no squealer. Give a man a chance to take his freedom anyway he can. You don't like jail, do you?'

Bass smiled.

'What the hell, we're just jumpy. Forgit it, Jim. You been damn good to all of us. Let's eat.'

But Bass and Barnes both kept a close watch on Murphy. It was next to impossible for him to file reports. Finally he did get one through to the sheriff.

They reached the vicinity of Round Rock on July 14. The next night they moved their camp nearer the part of Round Rock called Newtown, near some Negro quarters, south of the cemetery. They remained at that location, taking frequent trips into the town to view the bank, and to analyse the chance of successfully robbing it. Bass finally outlined the plan.

They were all to go to the bank on foot, leaving their horses hitched in an alley. Barnes was to give the cashier a five-dollar note to change, and while he was doing this Bass was to go behind the counter and level his revolver at the cashier and force him to hold up his hands, then Barnes would jump over the counter, take the money, and put it into a sack. In the meantime Jackson and Murphy were to stand in the doorway to keep anyone from coming in. After getting the money they were to move out along the San Saba road a short distance, then turn to the right and make their way to Denton, where they proposed to kill Deputy-Sheriff Wetsel and Constable McGintie of Denton County. They swore also that Billy Scott, the witness, should die, if they had to ride boldly into Dallas and fetch him.

The time of the holdup was set for a few minutes before closing time, as the outlaws believed that all deposits would be made by then.

In the meantime Jones in Austin had received letters from Murphy. He sent for Lieutenant Reynolds, in command of a squad of Rangers at Lampasas, to meet him at Round Rock the next morning. Three men were also sent to Round Rock early in the morning of the eighteenth, and Major Jones followed on the first train.

Arriving at Round Rock he went to the post-office, expecting to find a letter from Murphy, but was disappointed. He then gave information to the banker that the Bass gang was in the area and proposing to swoop down on his establishment. He took into his confidence Deputy-Sheriff Grimes and Albert Highsmith.

At nightfall nothing had been heard from the band, and Jones feared they had passed on towards Austin. He dispatched notices to the authorities there to be alerted and also sent messages to the town of Hearne to place guards at all the depots intermediate to Austin from Round Rock. He placed guards at Round Rock depot and in the vicinity of the bank. Next morning he wired to Austin for Captain Hall, who arrived at 2 p.m. Later Hall wired back for some of his men, as it was feared that Lieutenant Reynolds might not arrive in time.

Major Jones was excited. The trap was set now, and for the first time the law was waiting for Bass.

At the Bass camp, the outlaws were getting ready for the raid on the Williamson County Bank at Round Rock. Friday morning dawned bright and hot and dusty. Bass ordered Murphy and Jackson to ride into town early in the morning and look for Rangers.

'I seen a couple of cowboys in there yesterday looked like Rangers to me,' he said. 'Go on in and check around.'

Murphy and Jackson rode into Round Rock, looked around and returned. Jackson was not suspicious, and Murphy of course agreed that the town looked safe. When the robbers arrived at Newtown, Murphy suggested they get some tobacco and grub, since the plan was to hit the bank the next day.

'I'll trot over and have a look around,' Murphy said.

Bass agreed.

Murphy knew that Jones and his men were in Round Rock waiting for the Bass gang to strike, and his work was now accomplished and he had one objective—to cut loose from the band before the shooting started. Once they realized they had been betrayed, Murphy knew, they would turn their guns on him.

As Murphy rode off, Bass, Jackson, and Sebe Barnes unhitched their saddle-bags and started down the street towards the store. They strolled leisurely, and were spotted then.

Hoke Grimes, Deputy-Sheriff of Williamson County, was leaning against a post in front of a saloon. He walked carelessly up to the three strangers.

'You wearin' a six-shooter?' he said to Bass.

The outlaw turned around.

All three men answered in unison, 'Yes!'

Then it started.

Bass, Barnes, and Jackson all drew simultaneously. Grimes stood helpless as two of them fanned their guns point-blank at him. Six bullets ripped through his body and he whirled away from them, arms outflung, and crashed to the floor, dead.

The streets were soon echoing with gunfire. Major Jones, who was coming from the telegraph office when the firing began, rushed up the street. He stopped, sizing up the situation, and drew his gun, yelling to the Rangers who were now coming into the area from every part of town. Jones rushed on towards the three robbers, waiting until he was within fifty yards before he started firing. One of the trio turned and sent a shot whistling over the major's head. It struck splinters from the building behind him as he returned the fire.

They vanished behind a building and Jones bellowed, 'In the alley!' to keep the Rangers in pursuit.

The street was alive with frantic people and wild bullets. Men were rushing to get under cover. Women and children were screaming and running.

As the three outlaws retreated down the alley a merchant fired at them from the back door of his store. They hesitated a moment, then sent bullets flying into the door jamb. That pause delayed them just long enough for a Ranger to leap into the mouth of the alley and cut loose at them. His first shot tore into the small of Sam Bass's back, and the outlaw chief gasped and twisted against the wall of the alley, firing back. Then he turned and staggered to the end of the alley where the horses were tied. Another Ranger dropped to one knee, threw the barrel of his pistol across his forearm, and fired as they attempted to quiet their snorting horses. Sebe Barnes stiffened, and his head smashed against the side of his horse. He turned and fell face down in the street, a bullet through his head just behind his eyes. Jackson grabbed his saddle-bag and leaped on his horse. With Jackson's arm around Bass, who was riding another horse, the two men dashed wildly from Newtown.

'Frank was holding Bass on his horse,' Murphy said later. 'Bass looked pale and sickly, and his hand was bleeding. He seemed to be working cartridges into his pistol. Jackson looked at me as much as to say, "Jim, save yourself if you can".'

A few moments later, when Murphy saw Jones passing by, he jumped up and halloed, but the Ranger did not hear him. Then he turned and walked over to Newtown, which was bursting with excitement. Sebe Barnes had been killed instantly, and the townsfolk were crowded around the spot where he had fallen, discussing his identity.

Murphy said, 'If that was the Bass gang, this must be Seaborn Barnes.'

'How come?' one of the townsmen asked.

'Well,' Murphy said, 'if he's got four bullet-holes in his legs—three of 'em in his right leg—then it's got to be Barnes. He got 'em at Mesquite.'

The people crowded around Murphy, convinced now that

he was one of the bandits. As they prepared to arrest him, Jones rode back into town. His horse had played out during the chase.

'Let go of that man,' he ordered.

Then he took Murphy to the jail, where the body of Sebe Barnes was carried and placed on the floor. Murphy looked at the dead man and wiped his mouth.

'That's Seaborn,' he said.

'Seaborn. That's Sebe Barnes, right?' Jones said.

'Yes,' Murphy said, 'that's right.'

Jones was of the opinion that the badly wounded man who got away was Sam Bass, and he was elated over the prospects of capturing Bass soon.

'He can't go far, not shot to pieces,' he said.

Two Ranger lieutenants had arrived in Round Rock soon after the fight. Lieutenant Reynolds too had come in shortly afterwards, and Lieutenant Armstrong followed that night.

At dawn the next morning several Ranger companies rode out of town. Sergeant Neville of Lieutenant Reynolds's command was riding with eight men. They rode out from the point where the trail had been lost the previous night and continued the pursuit with Deputy-Sheriff Tucker of Georgetown. About four miles from town they rode up on a rail-section crew working along the right-of-way, with a pack of mules grazing near the tracks. A man lay under a tree nearby, but the Rangers thought he was tending the mules.

'You seen anything of a wounded man hereabouts?' Neville asked the hands.

'That fellow under the tree over there's hurt,' one of them answered. 'Says he's a cattleman and he got shot up in a fight in town yesterday.'

Neville approached the tree.

When he was about twenty feet away, the man called out to him: 'Don't shoot. I'm unarmed and helpless. I'm the one you're looking for. I'm Sam Bass.'

Major Jones sent an ambulance wagon to the scene, and

Bass was carried into town. A doctor checked his wounds and shook his head.

'You're dying, Sam,' he said.

Bass just nodded his head.

The bullet had ripped into the small of his back and had come out the front of his body. He had lost a lot of blood, and his arm was shattered.

The Press quickly telegraphed the news of the Bass capture. In the original news story, published in the *Austin Capital* on Sunday, July 21, 1878, nothing was mentioned of the part Murphy had played in the capture.

With word that Bass had been captured flashing through the State, morbid curiosity seekers and those who idolized the outlaw leader flocked to Round Rock. They came to await the death of Sam Bass. Major Jones sat beside the dying outlaw, trying to get information to settle some of the obscure points of his activities.

'Have you ever been to Collins's house?' Jones asked.

'Nope.'

Then Jones put the question differently, 'Where did you first meet Will Scott?'

'At Bob Murphy's.'

'You saw him at Green Hill's, too, didn't you?'

'Don't remember.'

'When did you see him at William Collins's?'

'I don't remember. I never paid attention to dates. I was always on the scout. I only saw him three times.'

It was an important answer, since it fixed Bass at the Collins residence. But this was the only really important information Jones got.

'About the shooting in Round Rock,' Bass said. 'Grimes asked me if I had a pistol. Said I had, then all three of us drew and shot him. If I killed him it was the first man I ever killed.'

About noon on Sunday Bass began to suffer greatly. Jones tried to get him to talk about religion, but he shook his head.

'I'm going to Hell, anyhow.'

Sam had been doggedly clinging to the delusion that he would survive the awful wound dealt him in the Round Rock battle, but about twenty minutes before his death he turned to the doctor and said quietly, 'Let me go.'

A few moments later he turned to the nurse and gazed around the room.

'The world is bobbing around me,' he gasped.

He breathed deeply, trying to catch his breath, then went limp. Sam Bass, the outlaw, was dead. It was two minutes before four o'clock, July 21, 1878.

Two days later in the *Galveston Daily News* the story of Jim Murphy's Judas act was divulged for the first time:

Round Rock, July 22—Sam Bass died at two minutes to four yesterday (Sunday) and was buried this morning by the civil authorities, to whom the body was turned over by Major Jones. Rangers are scouting for Jackson, who, rumour says, is in the vicinity, probably lingering to hear of Bass's fate.

The last moments of Bass were easy. He refused to the last to inform directly of his confederates, and said to Major Jones, when asked questions about his accomplices: 'It is agin my profession to tell. If a man knows anything let him die with it in him.'

Dallas, July 22—The credit of the capture of Bass and a portion of his gang is given to Sheriffs Johnson and Everheart, who matured and urged the plan of arresting Murphy, releasing him on bail, and spreading the report that he had jumped his bond. The plan worked like a charm. Murphy, hunted, apparently sought the camp of Bass for protection, and whenever opportunity offered dropped information of the whereabouts and purchases of the gang to Johnson, Everheart, and Capt. Peak. The plan to rob the bank at Round Rock having been agreed upon, timely notice was dispatched by Murphy to Johnson at Austin. . . .

Frank Jackson, Hank Underwood, and Henry Collins escaped all efforts to capture them and were never brought to justice. But the lawmen were satisfied. They had ended the notorious career of Sam Bass and, with it, the reign of terror which had gripped Texas for more than a year. As for Jim Murphy, plagued by a deadly fear that Jackson would gun him down to avenge Sam's death, he stumbled into Denton County Jail one day and demanded the protection of the sheriff. Everheart permitted him to move into the jail and Murphy, who had turned traitor to escape a life of confinement, was driven behind bars by his own distorted mind. And he could not long endure his voluntary life of terror. One evening he calmly stepped into a deserted jail cell in Denton County prison and blew his brains out.

Bass was buried at Round Rock and a small monument was erected over his grave. Through the years souvenir hunters have chipped parts of the stone away, but the inscription still remains:

SAMUEL BASS
Born July 21, 1851
Died July 21, 1878
A Brave Man Reposes in Death Here
Why Was He Not True?

6 Rube Burrow

On a rainswept morning in 1886, eight years after the battle at Round Rock, the ghost of Sam Bass loomed from its grave and threw its filmy shadow across the Bellevue water station of the Fort Worth-Denver Railroad in Central Texas. For on that December morning a gaunt, thirty-two-year-old Alabaman started down the highway of crime, and before he was through he was to blaze a trail of death and robbery that rivalled the career of his idol, Sam Bass, in daring and ingenuity.

Reuben Houston Burrow, the Alabama train robber, was a hybrid criminal. He used the robbery techniques of the Daltons and Renos; he evoked the sympathy and respect of the Press much as Sam Bass had done; like Jesse and Frank James, he won admirers in five different States, who were ready to fly to his aid when the hot breath of the law scorched his back; and, like King Fisher, he created controversy even in death.

That morning at Bellevue two masked bandits held guns on the engine-driver and fireman. The train had stopped at the water-tank, several hundred yards from the station, and as it stood idling three other bandits went through the passenger coach and robbed each passenger. Oddly enough, they did not go near the express car, and within a few minutes they jumped off and dashed away on horseback. Detectives and railroad police studied the methods used by these thieves and were mystified that the messenger car had been left untouched. What was this, they asked, the work of rank amateurs?

The second challenge came seven weeks later at a station of the Texas-Pacific Railroad. As the early morning train rolled into Gordon two men jumped on to the engine footplate.

'Keep it rolling,' one of them ordered.

A mile or so down the track the two bandits marched the driver and fireman back to the express car and demanded admittance. The clerk refused, but a volley of bullets tore through the door and he quickly changed his mind. The bandits rifled the safe of several thousand dollars and the same amount in United States registered mail. Then they were gone, riding splendid horses.

A posse was quickly formed and followed, but they were back within a few hours.

'These ain't amateurs,' the sheriff said. 'They went out aways north, then back-tracked south and cut off. We rode over their trail going out and lost them.'

From evidence gathered the Pinkertons decided the train robbers were the same who had robbed the Fort Worth-Denver at Bellevue. They frankly admitted they had no idea who had started what looked like the beginning of a series of daring train robberies. All they could do was to wait for the bandits to try again. But months went by.

Soon after the daylight attack on the Texas-Pacific at Gordon, a roughshod Alabaman bought a small ranch in Central Texas and settled down. He was Reuben Houston Burrow. With his wife and two children he soon earned the respect of the neighbouring ranchers. Burrow was a medium-sized man with a square-cut jaw, broad forehead, and a wide, firm mouth. He wore a short beard and his light-brown hair was long and unkempt.

A few weeks after purchasing the ranch, Burrow employed a young man named Will Brock to help him with the ranch work. Both men went about their business, ignored except for an occasional 'Hello' from a passing rider. All that was known about Burrow was that he was a native of Lamar County, Alabama, and had been born December 11, 1854, and in 1872, with a strong inclination to escape, he had left his native State to try his fortune in Texas.

He had married Virginia Alvison when he was twenty-two years old, and she had died four years later, leaving him two children. Four years after her death he had remarried, and now in 1886 he had settled down to an apparently peaceful life as a rancher.

What people didn't know was that Burrow was an extremely strong-willed man who possessed a marked degree of leadership; that he was one of the most deadly rifle and pistol shots in the territory; and that his ranch had been paid for with some of the profits of the Texas-Pacific robbery.

Early in May 1887 Rube's brother Jim visited the ranch with two of his friends, Nep Thornton and Henderson Bromley. Thornton was the gunman who had held up the engine-driver of the Fort Worth-Denver train while the other three robbed the coaches. Rube had sent for them because the quiet life at the ranch was making him restless. Accepting his ranch assistant Brock as a new recruit, he outlined plans for a new holdup.

'Where's it to be?' Jim asked.

'Gordon,' his brother answered. 'They'll never expect it there a second time.'

If Rube wanted to take the Gordon train again, then the Gordon train it would be—but the plot showed a lack of real planning on Burrow's part, since the slightest investigation would have shown that detectives were still hanging around. Luckily for the gang, the Brazos River rampaged a few nights before they prepared to cross it, and this spring flood thwarted their plan, so they returned to the Burrow ranch.

Two weeks later, on June 3, they set out again. This time they rode to Ben Brook, and Burrow looked over the surrounding countryside.

'Okay,' he told the band. 'This is it.'

A mile or two outside Ben Brook a long trestle bridge

All previous reward circulars issued by this Agency, referring to this robbery are annulled.

$700 REWARD.

REUBEN HOUSTON BURROWS, alias **RUBE BURROWS**, charged with highway robbery, having, with his brother, **JAMES BUCHANAN BURROWS, and others**, wearing masks on the night of **FRIDAY, DECEMBER 9, 1887**, boarded the north bound train on the St. Louis, Arkansas & Texas R. R. at Genoa Station, Ark., and compelled the messenger of the **SOUTHERN EXPRESS COMPANY** to surrender the keys of his safe, which they rifled of $3,500. **James Buchanan Burrows**, and three others of the robbers, **have since been arrested.**

In an attempt to arrest **Reuben Burrows and Jim Burrows in Montgomery, Alabama**, on January 23, 1888, **Reuben Burrows** shot Mr. Neil Bray, a compositor on the *Advertiser*, who had been called on and was aiding the officer in his arrest.

DESCRIPTION.

REUBEN HOUSTON BURROWS is about 32 years of age, 6 feet in height, weighs about 160 pounds, blue eyes which do not look a person full in the face, round head, wears 7⅛ hat, full forehead, face broad under the ears but thin near the mouth, short, inclined to pug-shaped nose, swarthy or sandy complexion, light sandy hair, thin light moustache, uses Hair Vigor to darken hair; left arm is a little shorter than the right, caused by having been broken at bend of arm; rather a lounging gait, carrying his hands in his pockets in a leisurely way.

Usually wears dark clothes and woolen shirts, a No. 8 boot, but no jewelry. Does not use tobacco; drinks, but not to excess; does not gamble, but can play the game of seven-up; is somewhat of a country story teller, relating stories of snake, dog and cat fights, etc. Is a good horseman, carries a 45-calibre pistol and is a good shot.

He was born in Lamar county, Alabama, is married, and has two children who are now with his father in Alabama. His wife is residing with her father, Mr. Hoover, at Alexandria, Alabama. He resided for 14 years in Wise and Erath counties, Texas; has worked for the Mexican Central R. R., and is a member of the Masonic fraternity.

The **Southern Express Company**, and the **St. Louis, Arkansas and Texas Railroad Co.** have jointly offered a **reward of Five Hundred Dollars ($500)**, and in addition **the Governor of the State of Arkansas** has offered a **reward of Two Hundred Dollars ($200)** for the arrest, delivery to the authorities of the State of Arkansas, and conviction of **Reuben Houston Burrows.**

Send information to

C. T. CAMPBELL,
Sup't Texas Express,
TEXARKANA, ARK.

Or to any Superintendent of
Pinkerton's National Detective Agency,
At Either of the Above Listed Offices
WM. A. PINKERTON, General Superintendent Western Division, Chicago, Ill.

Chicago, February 20, 1888.

Pinkerton's Detective Agency, the greatest of its kind, sent out numerous posters of this type as its agents tried to close the ring around the Burrow gang in 1888 crossed a deep gorge. Burrow and Bromley waited until the train was starting up from its stop at Ben Brook, then jumped aboard.

'Just keep it going,' Burrow said, waving his peace-maker at the crew.

As the train crossed the gorge Burrow snapped his orders, 'Haul it up so the engine's off the bridge.'

The train came to a stop at the edge of the bridge, the engine over solid ground, the rest of the train stretched out across the steel structure with a dead drop waiting for anyone who tried to get off. Jim Burrow, Will Brock, and Nep Thornton crawled over the wood tender, and split the messenger-car door with a coal-pick. The messenger stood rooted, staring into four guns in the hands of Thornton and Brock, while Jim took three thousand dollars out of the safe.

The five men jumped off the train and disappeared into the bushes. A few moments later the handful of passengers chasing them heard horses thrash through the brush.

'Get back to Ben Brook and rouse the sheriff,' one of them cried.

Before they could get the train back, however, their faces were pelted with raindrops, and within a few minutes they were bathed in a raging storm. In the hills the robbers hauled in their reins and stopped for a moment as Burrow looked up into the rain with a grin.

'I counted on this here rain,' he said. 'It'll wash our tracks out so clean no posse'll know where to turn.'

The Pinkertons were more confounded than ever. Since train robbery was a risky business, carrying a heavy penalty, they were fairly certain that the same gang had pulled the new holdup. The railroads were demanding action, and the detective agency bitterly ordered a sprawling investigation into the activities of every known thief and con man in the State. The investigation turned up nothing. The frustrated detectives were still hard at work three months later in September, when they were shocked by a new attack.

Two men boarded the Ben Brook train in the same place,

and the engine-driver and fireman were the same who had been running the train during the last raid.

'Well, I'll be damned,' said one of the masked men, recognizing them. 'Lookee here! Okay, gentlemen, you know what to do.'

The crew, resigned to their fate, shrugged and ran the engine to the edge of the bridge. Three other masked men scrambled aboard, and a few minutes later the five men vanished into the brush with the same amount of loot—three thousand dollars.

'Shall we head back to Ben Brook?' the fireman asked as the sound of horses echoed back.

'What's the use?' said the engine-driver, pointing to the sky. It was beginning to rain.

While Pinkerton detectives frantically started overturning every underworld rock in Texas all over again, Rube and his family and brother paid a long overdue visit to their former home in Vernon, Alabama. It was a wonderful reunion, for there were five brothers and five sisters: a tightly knit family. For two months the bandits strolled the county square and enjoyed a vacation, while detectives back in Texas continued to run into blank wall after blank wall.

Thus far the Burrow raids had been spaced about two months apart, long enough to let the trail grow cold and to confound the law. But in December Jim started back to Texas, looking for their next target. Soon after they crossed the Texas border they decided on the station at Genoa, a few miles from Texarkana.

The gang was ready for action, since two months had depleted their swag. This time they used a tactic employed by the Reno and Bass gangs. Two outlaws went up on to the engine as the train stopped for water and ordered the driver to run slowly down the tracks. About a mile from the station they had the train stopped and tried to get into the express car. The clerk steadfastly refused to open the heavy door, even after they poured shots into it.

'Okay, get the fireman,' one of the gunmen yelled. 'We'll burn him out.'

When the fireman arrived at the car with a burning stick of firewood, the clerk finally surrendered and unlocked the door. The robbers ripped the safe open and sped to safety with several thousand dollars.

This robbery stunned the officials of the Southern Express Company.

Sheriff Dixon of Miller County quickly organized a posse and Burrow tried a new ruse. Leaving the horses tethered in a gully, he and two of his men casually walked back to town, hoping to be ignored until after the posse was a good distance out of town, when they could ride in the opposite direction. But as the sheriff rode towards the three men on foot he yelled out for them to stop and put up their hands.

'He's on to it, boys,' Burrow growled. 'Let's give him some hell.'

The three bandits jumped into a gully, drew guns, and opened a withering blast of gunfire at the lawmen, who leaped from their horses and returned the fire. For two hours, until dark, the shooting continued, both sides managing to keep the other pinned to the ground.

Under cover of darkness the outlaws slipped from the gully and made their getaway. But the sheriff found a raincoat and a battered hat in the ditch where the men had been hiding, and the engine-driver identified the apparel as having been worn by one of the holdup men. It was the first clue uncovered in the series of five train robberies.

Pinkerton and special railroad detectives were given the clues and ordered to turn up something concrete. Finally, when an inquiry was made at Alexander, a shop assistant recalled selling the clothing to a man named Brock, who said he had come from Alabama. The detectives soon located Brock's home and established that he had been seen in Texarkana prior to the robbery.

Another officer in Waco had for several weeks been following a man with a reputation as a free-spender, and that man was William Brock. Comparing notes with the detective who had uncovered the evidence in Alexander, the Pinkertons were now certain that Brock had participated in the Genoa train raid. Further investigation revealed that Brock had two friends, Rube and Jim Burrow, who also seemed to be well heeled.

The agency shadowed Brock, expecting him to lead to the Burrow brothers. Another Pinkerton man, however, came up with evidence that the Burrows were in Alabama. Brock was taken into custody on December 31, 1887, at his home near Dublin, Texas, just twenty-two days after the train robbery at Genoa.

Under heavy guard he was taken to Texarkana, where the engine-driver of the Genoa train identified him as one of the thieves, and several citizens of Texarkana stated he had been there before the robbery. Confronted with such damaging evidence, Brock broke and confessed his part in the holdup. He also described the roles played by the Burrow brothers. Although Brock received a twenty-year prison sentence, it was a much lighter sentence than he would have drawn if he had not supplied the authorities with important information.

The Pinkertons dispatched three detectives from Texarkana to Lamar County, hoping to catch the Burrow brothers off guard and capture them without incident. These detectives planned to draw the two men out into the open without arousing their suspicion, but the Burrows didn't appear in town.

On January 10, 1888, at 2.30 a.m., a sheriff's posse started for the Burrow house. Fate stepped in on the side of the Burrow brothers, however, for the deputy missed the place in the darkness.

They surrounded the wrong house and by the time the posse moved down the road towards the Burrow house dawn was breaking. One of the Burrow family spotted the sheriff and detectives and awakened Jim Burrow, who, ironically, had decided to leave that day anyway. He quickly dressed and, evading the posse, spread the alarm. So Rube and his guilty brother escaped the posse and for the next three weeks lived on the run. Friends and relatives in the county readily sheltered them, and the law found it difficult to get any lead to their whereabouts.

By the end of the month, Rube and Jim decided to leave Lamar County. Posters describing them had been distributed throughout the South, and an alert train conductor named Callahan spotted them as they boarded the *Louisville and Nashville.* Callahan noted that the destination of the outlaws' tickets read Montgomery, Alabama, the State capital in fact, boasting a police force able to cope with the Burrow brothers. The conductor sent a message to Chief of Police Gerald at Montgomery. It read, 'Believe two men who boarded my train at Brock's Gap are the Burrow brothers.'

Captain John D. Martin was waiting when the train chugged through a driving rainstorm and stopped at the Montgomery station. The conductor pointed the Burrows out to the officer, who called for the assistance of the depot detective. Both officers were dressed in raincoats and slouch hats and created no suspicion when, as loitering citizens, they greeted the Burrow brothers and hospitably asked their destination.

'We are timber men,' said Rube, 'and want to get into the woods quickly. But we'd better get to a hotel in this weather.'

'We can show you some of the small hotels uptown. Come along with us.'

Rube and Jim could not chance arousing the suspicions of the two men by refusing to join them, so they followed. The four had walked about half a mile when the officers stopped in front of a dark building. As the officer was inserting the key in the lock Rube asked, 'What in hell place is this?'

'You're at the jail, and you're under arrest, Burrow,' the detective answered.

Rube moved fast, struck out at one of the officers, leaped off the jail steps, and rushed up the rainy street. Jim tried the same move, but was dragged down by several police officers.

Others ran after Burrow as he raced away. The wily outlaw turned one corner, leaned against a wall, and fired as a group of police and citizens rounded the corner behind him. One man stiffened and fell dead in the gutter. The chase broke up in screaming confusion, and Burrow disappeared.

Back at the jail, Jim Burrow steadfastly refused to tell his name or answer any questions, but as the night dragged on the detective slowly broke him down.

Finally he told them: 'I'm Burrow—Jim. The other fellow is my brother, Rube.'

The streets were now alive with police. Instructions were to bring in Rube Burrow dead or alive. While the questioning of Jim Burrow continued, the search for Rube Burrow went on. The surrounding country swarmed with men of all ages anxious to pursue the fugitive. Even young boys, coloured and white, joined in the chase.

Just before dark the day following Rube's escape, two officers named Hill and Young had searched a Negro family's cabin about five miles south of Montgomery, but to no avail. Rube had been watching them. Shortly after the officers had left the place, Rube walked in and asked for some food. One of the young Negro boys had seen Rube. He dashed off after the two officers, and informed them that the man they wanted was at his father's cabin.

'Go in and tell him to come to the door—somebody wants to see him,' Hill said, after making a cautious trip back to the vicinity of the cabin.

The boy entered the house and told Rube that he had a friend waiting outside. Burrow guessed at once the police had discovered his hiding-place. He drew his pistol and leaped through a window. Young squeezed off both barrels of his shot-gun at the fleeing bandit, but the gun was loaded with bird-shot and was not effective. A farmer in the neighbouring house heard the commotion, came to the door of his house, and raised a rifle at Burrow as he rushed out of the bushes at him. Burrow, always the fast thinker, dropped quickly to one knee and pointed his empty revolver at the farmer, who immediately dropped his rifle and dived to the ground. Burrow was on his feet at once and into the tangled vines near the farmer's barn.

The two officers plunged after him into the swampy lowlands on the outskirts of Montgomery. The chase led through knee-deep swamps and creeks. The two officers, their feet frostbitten, returned to the city, while Burrow crawled out of the swamp, teeth chattering, and sneaked up beside a Negro cabin. When he was sure that the family was asleep and no one was lying in wait to ambush him, he crept into the house, sat for nearly an hour beside a smouldering fire, took what clothing he needed, and left.

Burrow stole a horse, rode hard until daylight, then released the animal and set off afoot through the Alabama River lowlands. The detectives were unable to find any trace of him.

Determined to rescue his brother, who faced a stiff penalty after Brock's confession, Rube returned to Lamar County and made vain attempts to locate Joe Jackson, the only living member of the Sam Bass gang. When these efforts failed, Burrow, through a letter written by his brother-in-law, contacted Lewis Waldrip, a gunman of notorious courage, who answered the summons to join the gang.

Burrow wanted to associate himself with the old Bass gang, so he allowed Waldrip the *alias* of Joe Jackson, and the two of them kept on the alert for the time Jim Burrow would be moved from Lamar County to Texarkana. For several days they hid out in a lumber camp, and egotistically Rube chose to bring up his own name during after-dinner camp-fire gatherings, then to sit back and gleefully listen while the lumbermen talked about 'that daring outlaw'.

They missed the train by seconds, and Rube was heartsick that he had failed in this attempt to rescue Jim.

He and Waldrip found themselves jobs in Tate County as farmhands, and they kept track of the progress of Jim's trial. Confronted with Brock's confession, Jim at first pleaded guilty to the charges, but people back in Lamar County raised money for a lawyer. Therefore, upon receiving legal advice, Jim changed his plea, and there was hope he would win acquittal. But he never even went on trial for, on October 5, 1888, a few days before court convened, he died in jail of a fever.

Rube was crushed by this news. He felt in his heart that, if he had not been too late to meet the train that morning at Arkadelphia, Jim Burrow would never have died so young. This was an obsession which gripped him until his death.

During the next two months it seemed as though the earth had opened and swallowed Rube Burrow. Then, ten days before Christmas, he struck again, and this time his holdup was to launch the bitterest efforts so far exerted by the authorities.

At a few minutes before midnight, December 15, an Illinois Central train was pulling slowly out of the Duck Hill, Mississippi depot, when two men darted out of the shadows and leaped aboard. The engine-driver, Albert Law, at first believed the men were tramps.

But one of them pulled a six-gun and snapped: 'This is a holdup. Keep the train moving. Don't make a sound. All we want's the stuff in the express car.'

Law kept the train moving about a mile down the tracks, then was ordered to stop it. At gunpoint he and the fireman led the way back to the express car, where the Southern Express messenger, Harris, was forced to open the door. The larger of the two bandits entered, held his pistol against the man's head, and told him to open the safe.

Further back in the train, Wilkerson, the conductor, realized that a holdup was in progress. He found a volunteer in Chester Hughes of Jackson, Tennessee, who was travelling with his widowed sister and her two children. Wilkerson and Hughes armed themselves with Winchester rifles and crawled to the top of the passenger coach. They spotted one of the outlaws crouched in the darkness outside the express car and opened fire. Their bullets whined past his head and he climbed into the wood tender and answered their fire. Inside the car, the other outlaw quickly emptied the safe of about two thousand dollars and then joined his confederate. Working his way around the edge of the car, he got Hughes in his sights and squeezed off three quick shots. All three bullets ripped through the young man's stomach and he fell screaming on the roof of the car. He died quickly.

The two outlaws jumped off the train and made their getaway, while Wilkerson fired at their retreating figures.

News of this holdup and of Hughes's murder spread like a prairie fire, but once again the robbers successfully evaded all attempts to capture them.

Rube Burrow was now a man with two murders chalked against him as well as half a dozen robberies. Rewards had been posted and at least five different law-enforcement agencies were on his trail; yet he returned to Lamar County. In his home territory he took it easy and worried little about being arrested. The people looked upon Rube with some sort of admiration, especially his relatives. Rube knew how to handle them. With a lavish hand he distributed gifts of money, watches, and jewellery.

Pinkerton Detective McGinn was a shrewd operator, but he failed to realize the influence of the Burrow clan in Lamar County. Everybody for miles around knew Rube Burrow and his family, which through marriage and intermarriage had spread like a huge spider's web over the whole region. These illiterate backwoodsmen were as cagy as a fox and suspicious of all 'furriners'. Every move made by the law was carefully watched and signalled to Rube in one of his various hideouts. All inquiries for a guide to lead the officers back into the hills got the same reply: 'Lawsey me, I don' knows nothin' 'bout takin' yo' all. I hain't been ter the hills fer yars.' No one seemed to know where Rube Burrow's family lived.

Once a detective named Jackson shadowed Rube's brother-in-law, Jim Cash, for two days and finally spotted him putting a tempting dinner inside a hollow log. The officer hid nearby and waited for Burrow to claim his meal. An hour passed. Then a rifle-shot rang out and a few minutes later Cash appeared and placed a red cloth over the log. Jackson knew he had been discovered, although he was sure that Cash had not realized he was watched while he placed the dinner in its hiding-place. Evidently the crafty Cash had circled the entire area and fired a warning.

Detective after detective was frustrated in attempts to catch the elusive Burrow. The bandit remained at large while the angered lawmen tried to trap him, realizing he was almost within arm's reach.

Burrow meanwhile was planning his next move. He had always worn a mask in previous train hold-ups, but now he was plotting something new, for he saw a magazine article advertising wigs and false beards. On June 1, 1889, he sent money to a wig firm in Chicago with an order for a light red short-cropped wig and a beard to match. The return address was W. Gain, Sulligent Express Depot, Lamar County, Alabama. When the package arrived it had split open due to rough handling and improper packing, and part of the wig was showing through the side of the box. Moses Graves, the postmaster, was a nosy man and promptly forced the crack wide open so that he could peek at the contents.

When Jim Cash arrived to claim the package for Burrow, Graves refused to give it to him.

'Can't deliver it to anyone but this Mister Gain,' Graves said.

Angered, Burrow himself went to the Graves store, which also served as the post-office, but he got there after Graves had closed for the night. He rapped on the glass door and demanded the package.

'I'll give it to Gain and nobody else,' Graves yelled.

Burrow pulled his gun, jammed the barrel through a pane, and shot Graves down. Unlocking the door he grabbed the package and fled.

The wanton and cold-blooded murder of such a respected citizen as Moses Graves caused many indignant farmers and merchants to take up arms against Rube Burrow and his outlaw cronies. Sheriff Pennington, who had retired, donned a badge again and directed the raiding parties.

'Men, we've got to stop the Burrow outlaws once and for all. What kind of men are we anyway, allowing that cut-throat to roam free and easy in Lamar County? This is the time to stamp 'em out.'

Everybody agreed to that and soon a number of Rube's relatives and friends were put under arrest in an effort to learn the outlaw's whereabouts, but to no avail.

The murder of Graves spurred the officials of the Southern Express Company to renewed energy.

Detective McGinn arrived with a posse of Pinkertons to join in the hunt. However, it was as difficult as before to secure the assistance of a capable guide, for Rube's close friends and relatives still assisted him. Finally McGinn threw caution to the winds and headed his men into the thick woods without a guide. Once in the tangled woodlands, they soon recognized the hopeless task before them, as day after day they floundered around so confused that they doubted their ability ever to get back to civilization. The few miserable cabins they came upon were tenantless. Their supply of food ran out, and every man was covered with insect bites, scratches, and cuts. The 'outsiders' at last admitted defeat and made their way towards Vernon.

On the ride back McGinn and his men ran across an isolated cabin and decided to investigate. They suddenly changed their minds, however, when several slugs came crashing at them through the thicket. It so happened that this old cabin was a relay station used by Burrow to cache food against emergency, and only minutes before the posse's arrival Rube Burrow and Joe Jackson had arrived there. The cabin was old and in many places the clay chinking between the logs had fallen out, making fine loop-holes. This enabled the besieged outlaws to cover all sides efficiently. Trapped for the present, the outlaws kept up such a barrage that the lawmen dared not show themselves.

Darkness settled with the men still held in the cabin and the manhunters unable to flush them out. One end of the cabin had no door or window, so McGinn distributed his forces to cover the other three walls only. During the night Rube and Jackson were busy. While one patrolled the one-room shack, the other devoted his time to digging a tunnel under the wall on the blind side of the cabin. At dawn McGinn found his quarry had disappeared.

But Rube soon realized that he had to flee that part of Alabama. With every house under surveillance and Pinkertons streaming into the county in search of him, Rube knew his luck could not long endure. He sent Jackson on ahead, promising to meet him again near the Lamar County line.

'I've got to get a new recruit and think I know just who,' he told Jackson.

For months rumours had been inferring that Burrow's cousin, Rube Smith, was a spy in the employ of police officers. Smith had been a reputable citizen until late in 1888, when he helped rob a wealthy farmer. Arrested and indicted, Smith had escaped from jail and for several months had been in hiding. Burrow was not sure whether Smith was a Judas working to cancel his own debt to society or whether the rumours were unfounded, and Smith might of course become a valuable member of his small band. He sent Smith a note asking his cousin to meet him in a lonely graveyard, and during this meeting he became convinced that Smith was as desperate as himself.

'We've got to leave Lamar,' Rube told his cousin. 'This county's crawling with railroad badges and squealers. It ain't safe any more.'

The two men joined 'Joe Jackson' Waldrip and headed for Buckatunna, Mississippi. Several months earlier an officer for the Mobile and Ohio Railroad had boldly stated during a newspaper interview that Burrow would never raid his railroad. Burrow had heard the challenge, and now he was on his way to prove that the Mobile and Ohio was just as easy a target as the other railroads he had looted.

Burrow's original plan was to hold up the train at Ellisville, but, *en route* to Buckatunna from Ellisville, the three bandits had to cross Buckatunna Creek, and here Burrow noticed a trestle bridge beyond the trees as he was riding through the shallow water. He immediately changed his plans.

Leaving Waldrip, he and Smith returned to Buckatunna to await the arrival of the train. At 2.15 a.m. on the last Wednesday in September 1889, as the train pulled into Buckatunna station, Burrow and Smith jumped aboard. Brandishing their six-guns they told the driver, Zack Therrill, to stop the train on the bridge so that the passengers could not alight and chase them.

The train hissed to a stop as the engine, tender, and express car rolled over solid ground. The bandits quickly rifled the safe. Then Rube ordered Therrill to pull the mail car off the bridge. The two Rubes went through the registered mail, then rushed to their horses and made their getaway. They had collected four thousand five hundred dollars.

As soon as the news of the hold-up reached the railroad and express officials at Mobile the return telegraph messages hummed with excitement. Engine-driver Therrill was advised to hold his train at the scene of the robbery as a special engine carrying detectives and bloodhounds was speeding from Mobile to the scene of the holdup.

By early morning a large crowd of armed farmers and merchants had gathered around the members of the train crew. About the same time the special from Mobile lumbered in. Soon the detectives had selected a formidable posse from the ranks of the local people. The robbers, no doubt, had anticipated the use of the bloodhounds in the chase and threw them off the scent by taking to many of the shallow streams in that vicinity. The dogs were of little or no use. The posse grew discouraged as the trail grew colder, and, exhausted, most of the men dropped out and returned home. Several determined detectives, however, persisted.

At Demopolis, Alabama, they uncovered an important clue.

As in the case of many of the West's famed outlaws, Rube Burrow and 'Joe Jackson' Waldrip had a tendency to return to their birthplace after each robbery. Rube Smith had left the trio a few days after the robbery and returned to Lamar County by train, arriving October 5. A brilliant detective named Thomas Jackson, by means of a description of the third man, had deduced that he was Burrow's cousin. His suspicions were confirmed when Rube Smith returned to Lamar County and started spending money like water.

Rube Smith had heard through the grapevine that the detective was on his trail. Joining with a gullible weakling named James McClung, whom he had lured into the outlaw trail, he fled West towards Indian country. They were planning to rob the Indian Agency office *en route*, but a sheriff, on the watch for Smith because of his previous crimes, recognized him and opened fire on the outlaw pair as they rode towards their goal. They returned in haste to Lamar, where they could rely on the local people to help them.

It was a cold and dull December noon when Rube Smith and Jim McClung walked into the tiny station at Amory, Mississippi, and huddled up to the pot-bellied stove to thaw out their weary bones. They expected no trouble as the place was occupied by only a tired-looking old man with over-sized eye-glasses.

'Ticket?' the old man asked.

'In a while, we want to rest first,' Smith grunted.

Neither man was prepared for Detective Jackson when he rushed into the small room, accompanied by two policemen. McClung made no resistance, but Rube Smith flew into a wild rage and attacked Jackson. The police quickly subdued and handcuffed him. A police wagon took the prisoners to the jail at Aberdeen, Mississippi. On December 18, less than three months after the hold-up, McClung made a confession in which he stated that he knew Smith had taken part in the Buckatunna express car robbery. This confirmed the information which Detective Jackson already had in his possession.

Rube Smith cracked when faced with this evidence, and he admitted complicity in the Buckatunna affair. Taken to Waynesboro, Mississippi, on April 1, 1890, he was convicted and given the maximum sentence at that time, ten years in the State Penitentiary. McClung, who had assisted the State in obtaining damaging evidence against Rube Smith, got off scot-free.

Rube Burrow and Joe Jackson obtained a rest period when the police had a shoot-out with two moonshiners near Oneonta, Alabama, for the sheriff of Blount County was certain the two men were Rube and Joe.

Shortly after the capture of the two still-keepers, however, Lamar County again swarmed with police officers and deputies. It was not a safe place for Rube and his outlaw pal. Rube's father, Allen Burrow, advised a hasty exit from Alabama. Possibly a trip to Florida might do the boys a world of good.

To allay suspicion, the elder Burrow drove both men in a covered wagon, followed by Jim Cash with ox-drawn wagon, as far as Columbus, Mississippi. There the cart and oxen were turned over to Rube and Jim, who then continued south, while the elder Burrow and Cash returned to Lamar County.

The detectives in Alabama suspected that Rube was in possession of the cart and oxen, but Mr. Burrow spread the word that the rig had been stolen in Columbus. This only strengthened the belief of the authorities that Rube and Jackson had escaped with the cart. One of the detectives, working on that theory, went to Columbus. The man worked alone for two months; then the officer learned from a trapper who had come into Columbus that two men riding in an ox cart had been around Carrollton, forty miles away.

The officer quickly concluded from this information that

the outlaws were headed for Florida and probably would cross the Alabama River at Gainestown. He was right. A quick trip via the Louisville and Nashville Line to Gainestown confirmed the officer's belief. Two men answering the descriptions of Burrow and Jackson had crossed there several weeks before. It was tedious work. The detective went from point to point inquiring about the two outlaws. At a landing on the Yellow River he learned that the two men had separated and that Rube was working at a log camp under the name of Ward. He also learned that Ward came to the ferry-landing almost every day.

The officer wired railroad officials. On February 6, 1890, a force of officers and express police met the detectives at Broxton's Ferry and heard the story, and it was decided to wait at a ferry-crossing on the banks of the river where Burrow had to bring in a load from camp. They had been told, 'Order Burrow to surrender, and if he doesn't, shoot to kill.'

But once again Burrow's luck held. He didn't appear at the ferry-crossing for two days, and the lawmen had by then begun to work the ambush closer to the camp. They engaged the services of a local man to show them the route into the lumber camp, then ordered him to return home. But the man decided to trail along to watch the fun. His house stood along the route usually taken by Burrow when he went to town, and the outlaw stopped there for a chat. The man's nervous wife told Burrow her husband was out hunting. Her behaviour was enough to tip off the wily Burrow that something was wrong. Rube dashed into the woods and made a detoured trip to the log camp. He arrived there about midnight and had the cook prepare him some rations. He was not nervous or afraid but told the interested cook tales of outlaw adventure and daring, always managing to slip in the name of Rube Burrow. Several hours later he calmly walked into the woods and hid himself in a small cave. Rube was alone, but content with the knowledge that he had again outwitted his pursuers.

The posse returned to Lamar County with Burrow's wagon,

which was hardly worth the trip. They impounded the cart and sold it in Burrow's home town. Again his brazen nerve was exhibited. When the outlaw heard they had taken his wagon and sold it, he wrote out a bill of sale to a friend, who tried to retrieve the vehicle. The law refused to honour the bill, but were embarrassed at Burrow's flaunting.

Rube went south into Florida and took refuge in the swamps and backlands. The police were still concentrating on Lamar County, and their vigilance paid off, for 'Joe Jackson' Waldrip did return, feeling that his sojourn in Florida had thrown the law off his trail. Detectives watched his every move.

On the night of July 15, Waldrip and Jim Cash left the home of Rube's brother, Allen, feeling once again that Lamar County was unhealthful. The officers trailed along, careful not to be outwitted in a night gunfight. At Fernbank, Waldrip boarded a train and took a seat in the women's coach, apparently believing himself safer there. When the train rolled into Columbus, Mississippi, he stepped on to the rear platform for a breath of fresh air and was arrested by a dozen officers. Not a shot was fired. Heavily manacled, he was whisked to Memphis, Tennessee, there to make a full confession.

After his conviction Waldrip was taken to the State Prison, where officials attempted to connect him with Rube Smith, who was serving a term. Smith's confessions and Waldrip's still left many loose ends unexplained, but Smith refused to admit that he even knew 'Joe Jackson' Waldrip. He was planning an escape, and took Bill Moody, a fellow inmate, soon to be released, into his confidence and gave him letters to deliver to his father. In the letters Smith requested his father to find someone to climb the poorly guarded walls of the prison and supply him with guns and ammunition. Moody turned over his information to prison officials, and Smith was placed under double guard.

Meanwhile lawmen had succeeded in locating Rube Burrow in the Florida swamps, and once again he was on the run. This time he made his way to Santa Rosa County, Florida, near the Alabama line, and hid out in the area along the Gulf Coast. This was a thinly populated region at the time, with most of the less-than-ten-thousand inhabitants living in Milton, the county seat. The land was nothing more than canebrakes and almost impassable marshy bottoms, full of poisonous snakes and insects. In that desolate wilderness Rube met Lee Wells, a dissolute man who lived with his family in a ramshackle log hut in the densest part of the Florida jungles. Rube believed he had found a friend. Nonetheless Rube never trusted Wells, even refusing to live in the man's cabin, preferring to sleep outdoors.

In their search of the Santa Rosa swamps the detectives learned that Rube had spoken about a man named John Barnes of Baldwin County, Alabama. They also learned that Barnes had worked with the man named Ward in the log camp on Lovette's Creek, in 1888. A diligent search revealed that Barnes was living on a small farm near Castleberry, Alabama. A report of Ward's habits and description proved to the officers that Ward had in reality been Rube Burrow. Barnes was shocked, to say the least, and the detectives were able to convince him that his civic duty was to entice Burrow from the swamps so that he might be captured and brought to justice.

Barnes had been raised in the Santa Rosa district and knew the swamps well. However, he was unable to contact Burrow. He did run across Wells, though, and assured that individual that he was escaping from the law.

'There's another outlaw in hiding around here. You ought to make a deal with him,' suggested Wells.

'Yeah? Who is that?'

'Don't know for sure,' Wells lied, and Barnes knew he did.

'How about him meeting me here at your place soon?' asked Barnes.

Such a meeting was agreed to, but Rube saw through the scheme just as soon as Wells told him about Barnes's visit.

While Barnes was trying in vain to work up an 'outlaw' partnership with Rube, that daring bandit was planning another train robbery. He decided to try something which hitherto had been unheard of in crime annals—a single-handed train robbery!

On September 1, 1890, almost a year after the Mobile and Ohio job, a coarsely dressed man boarded the Louisville and Nashville train at Flomaton, Alabama, just across the State line from Florida, and near Burrow's hiding-place. Nobody paid much attention when he stepped into the coach next to the engine. The next thing the engine-driver knew he was peering into the muzzles of a pair of .45-calibre pistols. The man ordered the driver to take the train to the Escambia River Bridge and stop there, leaving the engine and express car over firm ground.

When the train stopped Burrow forced the driver and fireman to jump off. He ordered them to walk back towards the express car, but the fireman broke and ran into the timber. Burrow fired several shots at him, but missed. He turned quickly and made his way back to the messenger car, all the while talking towards the brush to give the impression that several bandits were hiding there. He forced the engine-driver to pound on the express-car door with a pick until it shattered. The messenger dropped his rifle when he saw Burrow's two pistols confronting him and stuffed all the money from the safe into the robber's sack. Then Burrow calmly walked off into the woods at a brisk gait. He made his way back to Santa Rosa County.

Never in the history of outlawry had the law been so flagrantly flouted. The peace officers of the entire South-east were humiliated by Burrow's precedent-shattering feat. The possibility of a lone train robber had been considered too ridiculous even to ponder. Barnes, unsuccessful in his first attempt to bring in the outlaw, was encouraged to lead the manhunters through the swamp to the Wells place. Orders were short and to the point.

'Bring in Burrow.'

'Shoot first. Ask questions later.'

'Don't give him any quarter.'

The party led by Barnes started on foot from a railroad station south of Milton, the county seat of Santa Rosa County. It was nearly forty miles from there to the home of Wells. It took the inexperienced swamp hunters three days to reach the point which brought them in sight of the Wells place. Another three days and nights were spent in a vigilant stake-out of the premises, without sign of Rube.

'He can't live without food,' one detective said, 'and he's getting it from Wells, no question about that.'

'By golly, a few more days of this swamp and bugs and rot and you can have Rube Burrow!' muttered a weary officer.

On the morning of September 18 the posse decided to take the entire Wells family in custody in order to cut off Burrow's food supply. The officers closed in on the cabin, but Rube was not to be found.

'There was a man named Ward hanging around here,' Wells said.

'Yes, and you knew he was Rube Burrow,' remarked Barnes.

'The hell I did!' snarled Wells.

As soon as the posse put in its appearance several of the Wells children walked about the premises, ostensibly carrying out their usual chores. In reality they left a warning for Rube that officers were about. This was a prearranged signal—a red ribbon tied to a large bush on the outskirts of the Wells clearing. While the weary officers waited in vain at the Wells cabin, Rube Burrow calmly walked out of the swamp and headed for Castleberry, the home of Barnes.

When Rube failed to appear for several days, the discouraged band of manhunters left the Santa Rosa swamp, firmly convinced the outlaw had had some warning. Crestfallen and chilled to the very marrow, the posse disbanded and headed for home. Several of the Express Company detectives, however, kept on the move towards Lamar County, in the hope that Rube would arrive there.

On September 29, Rube again showed his brass. He went to the home of Barnes. It was early in the morning and Rube asked for some breakfast. Barnes was at first afraid Rube was angered because of the police plot and had come seeking revenge. Barnes invited Burrow to be seated while he went into the kitchen to assist his wife with the meal.

'That's Rube Burrow, the outlaw,' Barnes told his wife. 'I've got to get help from the neighbours. He might try to kill me for leading the posse into the swamp.'

'I'll entertain him while you are gone, but hurry. He'll get suspicious in a little while,' Mrs. Barnes replied.

Barnes wrote a note for the Pinkertons at Mobile, telling them Burrow was at his home, gave the message to a neighbour's wife, and asked her to rush to Castleberry and wire it to Mobile.

He returned to his small, modest farmhouse. Barnes found Rube in a peaceful mood. The outlaw made no attempt to question Barnes about his part in the raid on the Wells cabin; in fact, he was quite friendly and only wanted a few supplies before leaving. Barnes furnished the outlaw with what food he could. Then without further ado Rube left the Barnes place afoot in the direction of Lamar County.

Immediately upon receipt of Barnes's telegram, detectives hastened to Lamar County on the chance that Rube might be heading in that direction. Others went to track him from the Barnes place. The officers surmised that the outlaw was making for his home town, and quickly set out to intercept him.

Seven miles from Bell's Landing, the officers requested the aid of John McDuffie, a fearless citizen who had been highly recommended by the sheriff of Monroe County. The landing was guarded all night and on the morning of October 3 it was decided that Rube had not yet crossed the Alabama River. At ten o'clock that morning news reached the officers and McDuffie that Rube was eating breakfast in the cabin of a Negro sharecropper on the McDuffie farm. Another coloured farmhand had brought the message from Mrs. McDuffie. The six miles to the cabin were covered at a fast ride, but it was too late. Rube had gone to the river, grabbed the only boat available at the landing, and rowed across the Alabama, forcing the posse to charge several miles downstream before they could obtain passage across.

The detectives hoped that Rube would leave the swamps and take to the open highways. They secured a covered wagon and rode towards Demopolis.

On Saturday, October 4, the posse reached Thomasville, Alabama, and learned that a man answering to Burrow's description had passed through there several hours before. It was agreed that McDuffie would search one side of the river; the officers the other side.

On October 7 a Negro named Jesse Hildreth saw smoke rising from the chimney of his cabin and walked in to find Burrow asleep. He awakened him before realizing that this was the most wanted outlaw in the States. The Negro kept calm, pretending he thought Burrow was just a down-at-the-heels traveller. Hildreth was an enormous man with arms like steel ties. He told Burrow he was looking for some lost cattle and even offered to sell him a horse. Together they went outside to look at the animal which was for sale and, while Burrow was looking it over, rain began to fall.

'Hell, let's not stand out here and drown,' Burrow said. 'We can talk about the horse when it stops raining.'

'Let's go up the way,' Hildreth said. 'A friend of mine lives up there. That cabin ain't much shelter, jes' like standin' outside.'

They went to the cabin of a Negro named George Ford to seek shelter until the rain died down. Hildreth stepped outside for a moment on the pretext of caring for his horse, and he told another coloured man named Marshall to locate some of the members of the posse and bring them to the cabin. Marshall quickly located McDuffie and one of the police officers, and they returned to the cabin and met Hildreth in the woods.

They decided to try to catch Burrow without any forewarning and thus avoid a chance of gunplay, so Hildreth and Marshall entered the cabin to attempt to disarm Burrow.

When they entered Burrow was seated near the fire, peacefully wrapping some of his belongings in waterproofed cloth. Hildreth offered to help him and, in walking past Burrow, knocked his rifle on the floor. As the outlaw leaned to pick it up, the huge Negro wrapped his vice-like arms around him. Burrow bucked and roared in anger, but Marshall leaped on him too, and the three men crashed to the floor. McDuffie and the police officer rushed into the cabin and levelled their guns on Burrow.

'We got you, Rube,' McDuffie said. 'You're through. Just relax.'

Burrow was disarmed and bound, and by nightfall he was in the county jail at Linden.

As in the case of other celebrated outlaws, the news that Burrow had been captured was greeted with disbelief. But the next day the *Mobile* (Alabama) *Register* carried the full story.

Demopolis, Ala., Oct. 7—This afternoon in South Marengo, Mr. John McDuffie and others, sent out by the Southern Express Company, captured the real, genuine Rube Barrow. As reported in the daily papers before, he was making his way back to Lamar County, had passed through Monroe, and has been in Marengo the past two days. . . .

McDuffie went to Linden jail this afternoon with Rube strapped hard and fast in front of him on his horse, being laid across, head on one side and feet on the other. His position was painful, but his captors could allow him no possible chance of escape.

The great Rube is now in jail in reality. He had only one hundred and seventy-eight dollars on his person. Mr. Agee and Mr. Fisher, superintendents of the Southern Express Company, are in the city, and will go to Linden to pay Rube a call tonight. Supt. Agee is greatly enthused over the capture of the long-sought and hunted Rube, and is the happiest man in Demopolis tonight.

The two coloured men showed great courage in making the

$7,500 REWARD

Murderers and Train Robbers.

The Southbound Express train on the Mobile & Ohio Railway was robbed on the morning of Sept. 25, 1889, by three masked men, who are the same parties who robbed the Illinois Central train on Dec. 15, 1888, and murdered Chester Hughes, a passenger, in so doing.

No. 1.—Reuben Houston Burrow, alias Charles Davis, is described as follows: About 34 years old, 6 feet 1 inch tall, weight about 170 lbs., light complexion, dark sandy hair, long drooping mustache, possibly chin and side whiskers of recent growth, inclined to be sandy. The eyes are blue, small and deep-set, giving the brow a protruding appearance; nose short and appears stubby. Teeth sound and upper front teeth project slightly outward. Lower jaws prominent and protrude noticeably backward under ears. Hair on top of head very thin. Head round. When spoken to generally throws head backward displaying Adams apple in replying to questions. Speaks abruptly and rather quickly. Right arm little shorter than left arm. Wears 7¼ hat and 7½ boot. He neither smokes nor chews. Has a habit of telling funny stories and also of quoting and ridiculing the Bible. Has small scar scarcely noticeable on forehead over left eyebrow, made by bird shot. Has a small mole on the right cheek bone. When last seen wore dark colored coat, gray jeans pants, and reddish brown slouch hat, with narrow leather band and leather binding, known as a cowboy's hat. Is very restless and always watchful.

No. 2.—Joe Jackson, alias Henry Davis. About 30 years old; 5 feet 8 inches high; weight about 165 lbs. to 170 lbs.; black hair, black whiskers and mustache, whiskers generally worn full but are thin on side of face. Dark complexion; eyes, black and round. Has noticeable scar on left side of cheek or neck, also scar high up on forehead, which he keeps concealed by wearing his hair banged over it. Manner reticent and avoids looking at one when talking. Frequently complains of rheumatism in lower limbs, and occasionally, especially in wet weather, limps, but the limping is caused by gunshot wounds and not from rheumatism. His body and limbs are covered with gunshot wounds. He is compactly built and has round face. When last seen, wore dark rough suit, with cutaway coat and dark slouch hat.

No. 3.—About 30 years old; weight, 145 lbs.; 5 feet 9 inches high; rather slim in build; black hair and black eyes; black mustache and whiskers, of recent growth; dark complexion, face rather long. When last seen, wore dark mixed clothing and black slouch hat.

These men are all coarsely dressed, and might be taken for farmers or country laborers. They carried two small dark satchels and rubber overcoats, and one or more Winchester rifles; also small bundle. All wore heavy pistols and leather belts with cartridges. Numbers one and two are generally found in company with each other, and pass as brothers, though they do not personally resemble each other.

The following rewards are offered for the arrest and delivery of the men who committed the robberies above named, and for their delivery to any one of the undersigned:

By the Mobile and Ohio Railroad and Southern Express Company, $2000.00.

By the United States Government, $1000.00 each.

By the Illinois Central Railroad Company and the Southern Express Company, $1000.00.

By the State of Mississippi, $500.00.

By the State of Arkansas and the St. Louis, Arkansas & Texas Railway Company, $500.00.

By the State of Alabama, $500.00.

Total reward, $7,500.00.

Wire or write information to D. McLaren, Supt., Mobile & Ohio Railway, Mobile, Ala.; G. W. Agee, Supt., Southern Express Company, Memphis, Tenn.; A. G. Sharp, Postoffice Inspector, Chattanooga, Tenn., J. G. Mann, Supt., Illinois Central Railroad, New Orleans, La.; H. C. Fisher, Supt., Southern Express Company, Nashville, Tenn., or the Governors of the above named States.

An especially large reward—equivalent to more than twenty-five thousand dollars today—was offered for the capture of the Burrow gang first steps towards capturing Rube. They will doubtlessly be handsomely rewarded. The whole amount of rewards for Rube is said to be thirty-five thousand dollars or more, of which McDuffie will receive a large share. . . .

People travelled many miles just to read the bulletins posted on the Burrow capture. Others streamed into Linden to see Rube behind bars. It was true: Rube Burrow was finally under lock and key.

At the time of his capture, Burrow had only one pistol on his person. He told officers the others had weighed him down and he sold them. According to McDuffie, his bag contained nothing dangerous.

At nightfall people began to leave the jail cell and return to their homes. Before supper Burrow's handcuffs were removed, but not his leg-irons. Several guards had been detailed to watch him, among them McDuffie and Jesse Hildreth. Burrow was so pleasant and relaxed they became suspicious and kept their eyes on him all night. The outlaw spent the night in a room in the jail and was not lodged in a cell.

Just before dawn Rube remarked to McDuffie that he was getting hungry.

'How about handing me my bag?' he asked.

McDuffie handed the bag to Burrow, who reached deep inside. Then the bandit suddenly straightened. McDuffie was looking down the barrel of a .45.

'Take off the leg-irons, Sheriff,' Rube ordered.

The dumbfounded lawman had no choice but to comply. Once free, Burrow made a strange request.

'Take me to Detective Carter,' he said.

Carter was the man who had led the particular posse which had narrowed down the search and actually squeezed Burrow into a spot where he had to surrender. Burrow's eyes smouldered with hate. He was out for revenge.

'I ain't seen Carter,' McDuffie said truthfully.

Actually Carter was asleep in a store nearby, a few hundred feet from where Rube Burrow was enacting the latest chapter of his stormy career. Burrow handcuffed McDuffie and at gun-point forced Jesse Hildreth to accompany him in a search for the detective. The odds were long against the outlaw. The town was overflowing with lawmen. Once out of the jail he couldn't hope to evade the law for long nor even to conceal that he had escaped. He meant to find Carter, however, and shoot him down.

While Burrow kept to the shadows, Hildreth made several inquiries about Carter. Somebody finally told him that Carter was spending the night in Glass's store. Burrow and Hildreth walked down the shadowed streets towards the Glass store.

'Tell Carter to come on out,' Burrow whispered.

Hildreth went to the door and knocked. Carter awakened and asked who was there.

'It's Jesse Hildreth, Mist' Carter. Can you step out here a minute?'

As Carter stepped to the doorway, Burrow leaped to his side and jammed his pistol against the deputy-sheriff's head.

'I want your money and rifle,' Burrow snapped.

Carter moved like lightning. Knowing that once he turned his possessions over to Burrow he was a dead man, the deputy reached into his pocket and pulled his .32-calibre revolver. Rube saw the movement, stepped back and fired a shot that slammed Carter back against the door jamb. The man fired as he lurched backward. Burrow's first shot ripped through his shoulder, shattering the nerves. Carter's gun roared four times at Burrow's retreating figure. The fourth bullet claimed its victim. It tore into the upper part of Burrow's stomach, severing the artery that leads from the heart to the liver. The outlaw gasped and crumpled to the ground.

Carter, whose right arm was permanently withered and crippled in his face-to-face duel with Burrow, was at once acclaimed a hero. It had taken a great deal of courage to draw and slug it out with the most dreaded bandit of the day. But the news of Rube's death was not cold before a storm of controversy clouded Carter's triumph. Opinions were expressed that Burrow had actually been murdered or lynched, and that the report of the duel was a farce. As in the case of King Fisher, the Texas badman, the newspapers were quick to pick up the spectacular discussion.

At 4.30 p.m. on October 8 a covered wagon drawn by four horses dashed up to the Demopolis railway station bearing the mortal remains of outlaw Rube Burrow. On the station platform two beer barrels were set on end and the coffin of rough pine boards was taken from the wagon and placed on them. The cover was removed and hundreds of men and boys filed past and took a first and last look at the bloody remains of the once-daring desperado. Not a sound could be heard, not a word was spoken as the awed onlookers passed the rude coffin.

The five-foot-eleven-inch, sandy-haired killer appeared ill-kempt, with a beard two inches long. His clothes were ragged and rough, indicating much wear and tear. The hole in his abdomen was plainly visible, many later stated.

Immediately afterwards, Burrow's body was placed aboard a Southern Express car which left Demopolis at ten o'clock that same night. All along the route from Demopolis to Birmingham vast crowds gathered at every station to see the train that bore the remains of the famous bandit. Many passengers on the train were permitted to visit the express car to view Rube's mortal remains.

At Birmingham more than a thousand persons gathered to see the body.

At eleven o'clock on October 9 the train reached Sulligent Station, Lamar County. There the coffin was delivered to Burrow's relatives in a rude and heartless manner—simply thrown from the express car, to fall where it may.

The *Birmingham Age-Herald* on October 12 published the following concerning the Burrows shooting:

Vernon, Oct. 10 . . . Rube Burrow was buried today at Fellowship, a quiet country churchyard several miles north-east of Vernon. His toes now turn towards the setting sun.

The manner in which his body was packed in a rude pine box, his clothing covered in mud, his long hair and beard matted and tangled, is a sad commentary on his capture. That was the condition in which his body was flung off of the Southern express car at Sulligent, at the feet of his aged parents and kinsmen. To say the least, this was an indication of heartlessness which bears a striking resemblance to the outlaw's own character. An exhibition of inhumanity that would put to shame Rube's most daring deed. The civilization of this day and time should have prompted at least a decent regard for the respectable old people and the inoffensive brother and sisters. From the source which condemned the notorious outlaw something more humane was rightfully expected.

Was the 'duel to the death' a reality? Whether it was or not, the following facts have developed since the arrival of the body in this county:

1. Rube was not shot. The only mark upon his body of that nature is a cut in his stomach, where the ball is said to have entered, made undoubtedly by a lance or penknife, a straight, narrow cut which any ordinary penknife could have made. There was no sign of blood upon his body or his clothing.

2. The most careful examination of his coat and shirt showed no sign whatever of a bullet-hole, or even a rent. It was an old and soiled garment, but substantial. A bullet could not have entered his body where the wound is, without passing through the shirt. The shirt is absolutely without a bloodstain.

3. His neck was horribly broken. A dark blue mark about an inch wide around his neck indicated death by strangulation.

4. Just above his left temple was a large bruise the size of a man's hand, beneath which the skull was badly broken. On the right of his forehead was a similar bruise. There were other bruises upon his body which might be accounted for by the struggle with the Negroes in his capture. The other marks cannot. A man with a broken neck and a broken skull could not have accomplished, after that 'scuffle with the coons', the remarkable feats attributed to Rube.

The fact is that Burrow's body was thrown from the train when it arrived at the station. Bloody, mud-spattered, bruised, the remains of the outlaw fell to the platform before his parents, a somewhat terrifying testimonial to the deep-seated hatred borne against Burrow by the law-enforcement officers. There is little doubt that Burrow had possessed courage, which evokes awe if not a certain amount of admiration. And the defilement of his body leaves little wonder that the Press championed the cause of the bandit-killer, vicious though he had been.

The law continued to badger 'Joe Jackson' Waldrip to force him to testify against Rube Smith. He was again approached on October 16, eight days after Burrow's death. Once again he flatly refused, reminding his tormentors of the scorn and hatred which others had suffered after betraying their outlaw partners or comrades. He told the officers to leave him alone.

On November 10, less than a month later, Waldrip—his real name was Leonard Calvert Brock, born July 13, 1860—leaped from the fourth floor of his cell-block while awaiting trial. Perhaps the reason he jumped to his death was that a few days earlier he had cracked and given a full confession of his complicity in the Burrow holdups.

Not long afterwards Rube Smith was tried for his part in the Buckatunna robbery. Although already serving a ten-year sentence, in Federal Court he was given a life sentence despite the efforts of a brilliant defence counsel.

As for Rube Burrow, his death even today remains a mystery. In retrospect, the report of his escape and death seems incongruous. It is strange that his bag had supposedly been searched and yet contained a pistol by which he could make his escape. It is equally strange that he was not lodged in a jail cell, but was kept in an open office guarded by two of the men who had effected his capture. There is a reliable report in the *Age-Herald* which left open the possibility that he may have been mobbed. On the other side of the argument, Deputy-

Sheriff Carter was permanently crippled in the reported duel which ended the life of Rube Burrow.

Whatever the truth, Rube Burrow was one of the last of the great outlaws, the only desperado ever to hold up a train single-handed. But his name now is dimmed by the legends which grew around such bandits as the James boys and Billy the Kid.

7 Billy the Kid

THIS savage biography is the story of William H. Bonney, Junior, Billy the Kid, the New York lad who grew up to become the most notorious gunfighter in the history of the West. It is also the story of a State, for the Kid's guns wrote a chapter in the history of New Mexico. For months his notched six-shooter formed a major barrier between that territory and its statehood.

Although it is true that the Kid did his share of cattle rustling, he earned his dubious reputation during the sanguinary Chisum-Murphy cattle war in Lincoln County, New Mexico. This bullet-spattered battle was so bitter that it resulted in the ousting of a territorial governor of New Mexico and a declaration of virtual military law. When the roaring guns were silenced, the Kid emerged from the gunsmoke smiling, unscathed, his own dreaded guns still ready for action. He was eighteen years old and had already chalked up an impressive list of victims on the handles of his various revolvers.

With the end of the Lincoln County war, the new governor, Lew Wallace—who later earned fame as the author of *Ben Hur*—offered the Kid a complete pardon if he would put aside his gun, but the youngster only smiled.

'If I put down my guns, I'd be dead within the hour,' Billy told the governor. On March 13, 1881, he wrote to Wallace:

199 Billy the Kid.

I have no desire to fight any more, and it is said I am called Kid Antrim, but Antrim is my stepfather's name . . .

(Signed) W. H. Bonney

It took Governor Wallace two years to silence those deadly pistols.

Bonney was born November 23, 1859, in Rivington Avenue, on New York's East Side, the son of William and Kathleen (sometimes called Catherine) Bonney. The record of his birthplace was obtained in the 1920's from the Kid's uncle, but hitherto has not been published.

Most accounts claim that the Bonney family moved from New York City to Coffeyville, Kansas, in 1862. However, the town of Coffeyville was not in existence at that date. It was not until 1869 that Mr. Coffey drove his wagon team with its first load of lumber from Humboldt, Kansas, to the present site of Coffeyville. Possibly those references are to the general location.

Sheriff Harvey Whitehill was the first man to arrest the Kid—on a stolen butter charge. The Kid's next offence was the theft of seventy dollars from a Chinese. He was again arrested by Sheriff Whitehill and placed in jail. The lad complained every day that his cell was too confining and that he wanted to exercise himself. The sheriff finally allowed him to remain in the corridor each morning for a limited time.

It was not long before the Kid found a way out of the jail. He simply crawled up the chimney, which was hardly larger than a good-sized man's arm. After that he began his career of lawlessness in earnest. The Kid might have turned out to be a good citizen, but his mother died in 1874 and his stepfather did not get along well with the boy.

What did the Kid look like about this time? He stood five feet, seven inches tall, weighed about ten stone, rather on the ungainly side, with sloping shoulders, hardly any chin, piercing eyes which were blue-grey and never at rest, but continually shifting and roving, much like his own rebellious nature. His weapons were a DA .41-calibre Colt's revolver and a Winchester carbine, .44 rimfire, commonly called a 'brass-jawed' Winchester. There was a peculiar facial characteristic that to an experienced manhunter would have at once marked him as a badman—namely, his shifting eyes and suspicious, arrogant smirk.

The Kid was a wanderer, carving his life out of the raw wilderness before he reached his teens. How he managed to survive after his leap from the jail roof has always been a mystery, for little is known of his life for the next few years except that he earned his living as a cowhand, and practised constantly with rifle and revolver. By the time he was sixteen his eye was deadlier and his draw speedier than those of any Old West gunfighter.

Later he was heard from at Camp Thomas, Arizona, where he killed a familiar character of the post known as 'Windy Bill', the blacksmith. In making his escape from that camp the Kid shot down in cold blood two soldiers herding the post's horses, selected the best one, and headed for Globe.

Billy became a close friend of Melquiades Segura, and the two opened a monte bank in Agua Prieta, Mexico, where business was good. It was the first time he had settled down. One night he was in a card game with José Martinez, a mean card shark, who suddenly shoved back the table, declaring the cards were stacked against him. His hand flashed to his holster. Bonney's hand moved like a snake. The gun seemed to jump, booming as it cleared leather. Martinez died with his hand on his gun-butt, a bullet through the heart.

A few nights later Bonney and some other men rode to the Mexican village of Mesilla. As they started out, Bonney was introduced to the others.

'Meet Billy.'

'Who?'

'Billy—the kid.'

From that moment Bonney was Billy the Kid.

The Kid's semi-official tally of twenty-one victims when he

died would probably have been doubled had it included Indians, for his deadliness with a six-gun was considerably sharpened by numerous scrapes with the Mescalero Apaches. One night the Kid and Jesse Evans rode into an immigrant party heading west through Mescalero territory and were invited to spend the night in the camp. Just as the sun began to set, the peace of the camp was rent with war-whoops as a band of Indians swept down on the wagon train. It was a short, brutal fight. Evans and Billy set up their rifles, drew pistols, and gunned down eight of the marauders while they were still charging towards the camp. The rest of the band wheeled and rode off into the hills, startled by the onslaught, and none of the whites was injured.

The next day the Kid was lounging in a small Mexican village when he learned that his friend Segura was being held in the jail at San Elizario, Texas. It was one of the Kid's nobler traits that he never deserted a friend.

That night Billy rode into San Elizario and rapped on the heavy jail door.

A fat Mexican answered the summons, and stared into the ugly snout of the Kid's pistol. Five minutes later Billy and Segura were on their way out of town, and the Mexican was reposing in Segura's cell.

Billy started north, and in Mesilla met Tom O'Keefe, a Texas cowpoke. They decided to make the trip together, but while they were crossing the Guadalupe Mountains a band of Apaches came screeching down on them. The two men pulled guns and gave a running fight. Billy's horse screamed and plunged over. With his mount shot from under him, the Kid pulled his rifle and crept from one mesquite bush to the next, killing redskins with both rifle and pistol fire. He worked his way into the protection of the hills and set up his defence.

As the Apache renegades rallied for an attack on his rocky stronghold, the Kid cut loose and several of the redskins were blown off their horses. They gave it up and rode away, and the Kid continued his journey on foot. A day or two later he made his way into Murphy's cow-camp at Seven Rivers, and there again he met Jesse Evans. This was the beginning of the fateful blood battle that was to rock the entire State and burn the Kid's name deep into Western legend.

During the growth of the great cattle ranges of the Southwest there were two rival factions in this valley. John Chisum owned the South Spring ranch, in the lower Pecos Valley, a beautiful spread with a rambling adobe house, always open to strangers with no questions asked, surrounded by cottonwood and fruit trees, roses and even species of birds transported from other regions. Here Chisum lived with his lovely niece, Sallie.

Not far away, in the shadow of Mount El Capitan, sprawled Lincoln, New Mexico, a raw frontier town controlled by a vicious political machine fashioned by the powerful and ruthless Major L. G. Murphy. Murphy owned a large store and a hotel, and he kept his steel grip on the city by means of hired gunmen, chief among whom were James Dolan and John Riley.

Like Chisum, Murphy was in the cattle business.

In 1875 two new actors entered the drama: Alexander A. McSween, a lawyer, who moved into Lincoln with his pretty wife Susan and was hired by Murphy to act as his attorney; and J. H. Tunstall, an Englishman who bought the Rio Feliz ranch, close to Lincoln.

And a third came—Billy the Kid.

Before long McSween and Tunstall became close friends, and they opened a large store to compete with Murphy. Since McSween was Murphy's lawyer and Tunstall posed no serious immediate threat as a cattleman, Murphy kept quiet. But storm-clouds began to swirl over the valley.

The Kid began work as a cowhand for Tunstall. He was eighteen years old, a happy, talkative lad with long, wavy, light-brown hair, sharp blue eyes, rather prominent front teeth and remarkably small hands and feet. By some he was considered a lady's man, by others a show-off. Everybody appreciated that he was an expert marksman. If Tunstall whipped off his hat, tossed it into the air, and yelled out to

Billy, the Kid unleathered his gun and put six shots through the scaling headpiece before it hit the ground.

A fight smouldered for several months before it exploded into open war with Chisum's accusation that Murphy was stealing his cattle. The Lincoln politico tried to hire McSween to defend several rustlers whom Chisum claimed to have caught in the act. A God-fearing, honest man, McSween lived by the Bible and not the gun. He was convinced that the Murphy riders were guilty, and therefore refused the case. Chisum heard about this and immediately hired McSween to prosecute the men. They were all convicted.

Murphy now turned his wrath against both McSween and his partner Tunstall. John Riley, a Murphy henchman, visited McSween one night on a supposedly friendly visit, but when he rose to leave a small gun which had been hidden in a secret pocket dropped to the floor. Riley quickly left the house, but his blunder was a stern warning to McSween that Murphy was out for blood.

Murphy decided to acquire Tunstall's Rio Feliz ranch and secured false attachment papers from the former owner. On February 13, 1878, he sent a twenty-man group of intoxicated gunmen riding out from his store to the ranch. Among them were Billy Morton, a deputy-sheriff, John Robinson, and three of the Kid's friends.

Tunstall, Dick Bewer, and Billy had been riding towards town, but the Kid and Dick went off into the foothills to flush game and do some haphazard hunting. The gunmen from Murphy's store rode up behind Tunstall and, without warning, opened fire on the defenceless Englishman. Bullets riddled his helpless body, and he jerked in the saddle and thudded to the road. The drunken assassins rode up and beat his body, then tied it to the carcass of his horse.

Billy and Brewer heard the blast of guns and rode to a rise. Helpless to assist their murdered friend, they sat and witnessed the wanton and useless beating.

Tunstall had been a close friend of the Kid's.

'Mark them, Dick,' he growled bitterly. 'Mark every one of 'em. They're gonna pay—to a man.'

Despite the Kid's terrible vow, the McSween-Chisum faction still attempted to play by the law's rules. They swore out warrants against the men implicated in Tunstall's murder and turned them over to Sheriff Brady of Lincoln County. It was a futile move, for Brady was on the Murphy payroll. McSween immediately saw Justice of the Peace J. P. Wilson and convinced him to appoint Dick Brewer a Lincoln County special constable.

A few days later Billy and several other McSween men spotted two of the killers patrolling the range. They chased these two men towards Rio Feliz and overtook them. On the way back to Agua Negra, the captives tried to break away. Seated on his horse a few yards away, Billy calmly drew his pistols and shot both men through the head. Then he hanged them from a tree as a warning.

On April 1, 1878, Billy the Kid gathered together five of Tunstall's deadliest marksmen and rode into town looking for the sheriff. In a side-street they hitched their horses and waited quietly beside an adobe building. An hour later, when Sheriff Brady came into town with the circuit clerk, Billy Matthews, and two deputies, Hindman and Peppin, they also hitched their horses and started walking down the street. The Kid and his gang stepped around the corner.

'Brady!' Billy yelled.

As the surprised sheriff and his men turned they were greeted with a deadly volley. Although the six Chisum men opened fire simultaneously only Brady and Hindman fell—Brady dead, Hindman mortally wounded. Peppin and Matthews managed to escape by running into an alley. While the gunsmoke still swirled, Billy calmly walked up and took Brady's rifle and pistol.

It was the most vicious and cowardly ambush in the annals of the Lincoln County war, but such were the Kid's tactics. He never took a chance when he didn't have to.

News of the murders was wired at once to the Executive Mansion in Santa Fe, but it would be a while before the Governor could actually put into motion any effective plans to combat the vicious Kid and his men.

The next victim of the war was a veteran of Indian fights, known as 'Buckshot' Bill Roberts, living at Blazer's Mill, in Ruidoso Valley. On April 4, 1878, the Kid was a member of a band which appeared at Blazer's Mill and had a brief but furious battle with its lone occupant. Roberts had expressed his desire to remain neutral, but it was not to be. As the Kid and the band approached the mill, Charlie Bowdre opened fire and placed a slug in Roberts's stomach. Roberts shot Middleton and also shot off one of George Coe's fingers. Dick Brewer, wishing to get in the final shot, poked his head from behind a woodpile and was instantly killed with a well-directed rifle-shot by the mortally wounded Roberts. When the Kid searched the body of Roberts he found a Dolan cheque for forty-seven dollars twenty cents made payable to Roberts.

Oddly enough, Roberts and Brewer were buried in the same coffin the next day. The leadership of the McSween followers then fell upon the shoulders of Billy the Kid. Although the actions of Brewer and his men have been criticized, they did have a warrant for Roberts's arrest, and were acting in an official capacity.

Governor Axtell in Santa Fe immediately tried to appoint a new sheriff of Lincoln County, but no one wanted the job. Finally George Peppin was persuaded to take the job on a temporary appointment. It was a dangerous job for anyone, especially Peppin, who was a staunch Murphy man. Peppin, of course, was not likely soon to forget the shooting of Brady and Hindman.

Peppin's official term started on June 1, 1878. Promptly he gathered a large posse and rode out after the Kid, trapping him at the Chisum South Spring ranch in the Pecos Valley. The valley exploded with gunfire, and the Kid and his comrades ducked for shelter. Before Sheriff Peppin could surround them, however, the Kid and his men were saved by the timely arrival of Chisum riders, summoned by a cowhand who had succeeded in getting past Peppin and his men.

Not until one afternoon in July did hostilities next come to a head. Billy and some of his men, including Francisco Semora, were visiting McSween, planning new strategy. Outside was the Mexican bandit, Chavez, an ally of the Kid's, with a dozen of his best marksmen, acting as rearguard. Word got to Murphy's henchmen that the whole Chisum faction was holed up in one spot, so they attacked the McSween residence. Twenty-five Murphy gunmen surrounded the house.

Deputy-Sheriff Turner in the rear yelled out: 'Billy! The house is surrounded. Come out with your hands up!'

Across the street in the Montana and Patron Houses, two hotels, more of McSween's men had gathered for battle. Murphy's gunfighters were hiding out in his own hotel and store, ready to fight. Gunfire burst out and bullets thudded against the adobe walls of the McSween home.

'The game is up,' the Kid said calmly.

His men rushed to the windows and answered the gunfire. The streets of Lincoln were alive with screaming bullets. Murphy dispatched two gunmen to the Montana and Patron Houses in an effort to reduce the effectiveness of the McSween fighters there. They succeeded in climbing to the roof of the Montana. But Fernando Herra, one of the best of Chavez's marksmen, took aim from nine hundred yards away and his first shot instantly killed one man, who crashed off the roof. The other turned and tried to clamber down, but Herra fired again, and he too plunged off the roof, dead.

Throughout the day Lincoln echoed with the roar of guns and the screams of the dying. A housewife sent a young rider for help, and by the next morning Colonel Dudley arrived from nearby Fort Stanton with several detachments of Negro soldiers and two Gatling machine-guns. Proving to be an alley of Murphy, however, he refused to stop the fight. Instead, he called a momentary truce and stepped in front of McSween's house. There he delivered an impressive speech suggesting that the Kid, McSween, and the rest of the men within the house surrender to Murphy. While he was speaking during the supposed truce two of the Murphy gunmen, Dolan and Hall, sneaked up to the rear of the house and set it afire.

The Kid ordered Mrs. Ealy, Mrs. Shields, and Mrs. McSween, who had entered the house during the night, to leave. Mrs. Shields and Mrs. Ealy ran to safety, but Mrs. McSween refused to leave her husband. When the colonel finished his speech the Kid realized the house was on fire. Flames licked at the walls, and smoke began to curl through the rooms. His answer was more gunfire.

Dudley then turned the Gatling guns on the Chavez men and sent them scurrying out of the city. The Montana and Patron Houses were riddled. The battle next centred on the McSween house, which was crackling with flames. The McSween men gradually were forced to withdraw to the kitchen, while the house burned around them. With only the kitchen of the large house intact, the Kid forced Mrs. McSween to leave. She stood staring at her husband a moment, then rushed out.

'Lady comin' out!' the Kid yelled.

Once Mrs. McSween was out of the burning shell, the battle began again, more violent than ever. The Kid decided they would have to make a dash for freedom. He turned to his old friend Semora.

'All right, *amigo*,' he said. 'Give it a try.'

Semora loaded up, kicked open the door, and rushed out shooting. He was cut down at the doorway. Two others dashed into a wall of lead and fell upon the growing pile of death.

McSween and the Kid stood in the doorway, death raging around them, death in front of them. The Kid handed the lawyer a brace of six-guns, but McSween shook his head.

'I've never used a gun, and I'll not start now,' he said.

He turned and stepped through the doorway, Bible in

hand, calling to Murphy as he did. Once again the firing-squad boomed and McSween twisted, gasping, as bullets tore at his body. The Bible flipped from his hand, and he slammed back against the wall. Another volley tore into him, and he slid down the burning wall and crumpled, dead.

Inside, the Kid turned to the remaining members of the gang.

'Damn them, let's go,' he said.

The rest of the McSween mob rushed the door, guns booming, and ran on to the patio, framed by the blazing remains of McSween's house. They rushed straight at the Murphy men, and for a brief moment two dozen men stood face to face, shooting one another to bits.

The Kid was the last to leave, six-guns in each hand blazing. He rushed through the Murphy line, leaving one man dead and two others writhing with bullet wounds. The entire story of this battle was described by a Mexican named Salazar, who was gunned down as he left the house and shammed death. He saw the whole thing, including Billy's calm demeanour and race to freedom.

Billy the Kid was still alive, but Murphy had won his war. Streets and hotels were littered with the dead and dying.

President Rutherford B. Hayes was so shocked by the horror of the fight and by the apparent prejudice of the law in favour of the Murphy faction, that he removed Governor Axtell from office and appointed Lew Wallace in his place. Colonel Dudley was severely reprimanded for not having used the Army to force neutrality.

The most ironic element of the whole brutal massacre was that Murphy, in whose name the battle had begun, had, a few hours before its start, died in Santa Fe, where he had been visiting friends. His régime, although victorious in this fight, was cracked. Members of the faction still roamed at large, but the powerful political machine had been shattered by its own greed.

When Governor Wallace arrived in Lincoln, he invited the

Kid to a meeting in the Ellis House. Billy obliged and came face to face with the new governor of New Mexico.

'Billy,' Wallace said, 'as long as New Mexico is a battle-ground for gunfighters and lawless renegades, the Legislature will never accept it as a State. Put away your guns, and we'll grant you a full pardon.'

The Kid refused, for he knew that Lincoln County was still crawling with Murphy gunmen itching to put a bullet in his back. He turned and left the Ellis House a wanted desperado.

Patrick Floyd Garrett, a former range hand, was conducting a small restaurant and general store in Fort Sumner, New Mexico, and he became a close friend of the speedy Billy the Kid, who often made trips to the store for supplies. Garrett was a native of Alabama, who had gone West after the death of his parents in 1869.

Oddly enough, it was Chisum, once a friend of the Kid's, who came between these two friends now. The rancher realized that times were changing and, if New Mexico could ever hope to become a State, men like himself with power and prestige would have to back the movement. Knowing that immigrants had heard the stories of Billy the Kid and the Lincoln County war, and were wary of moving into the county, he summoned Pat Garrett to Lincoln.

'You're a friend of Billy the Kid's, aren't you, Pat?' he said.

'That's right, Mr. Chisum.'

'So am I, Garrett. That's why I hate to say this. I want you to accept the sheriff's star of Lincoln County. There's only one man in the territory fast enough to stop the Kid. That's you.'

Garrett was stunned by this invitation to kill his closest friend. He refused and returned to Sumner. Garrett felt that Billy had been forced into his career as a gunman.

But the Kid was changing, for he no longer needed any excuse to kill.

Early in 1880, a few weeks after the meeting between Garrett and Chisum, a drunk named Grant was bragging in a Lincoln bar.

'Billy the Kid ain't so tough,' he said. 'I'll bet I can kill a man before he can. Before the day's over!'

'I'll take that money,' a voice said.

The Kid stepped up to the bar and covered the bet. Actually he was making the wager to humour the drunkard, but towards evening a friend of his walked up to him on the street.

'Word's around that one of Murphy's old boys is in the bar —Grant. He's gunnin' for you.'

Billy walked into the bar and saw Grant leaning at the rail. He walked up and playfully lifted Grant's gun from its holster.

'Nice gun,' the Kid said.

Then he noticed two empty cartridges in the cylinder. He clicked it around so that when the pistol was fired the pin would strike an empty shell. He slipped the gun back in its place on Grant's hip. Witnesses to this act carried the tale, and it later became the gulf between Pat Garrett and the Kid.

Grant worked up his courage and turned to face the Kid.

'We got a bet, remember?' he snapped.

The Kid stood smiling and answered, 'Sure.'

'Now's as good a time as any.'

Grant snarled and drew. He squeezed off his shot and the gun clicked harmlessly. His face paled. He stared down at the pistol in disbelief.

The Kid's hand flashed to his holster and his gun roared. The bullet smacked through Grant's neck and he fell dead at the Kid's feet.

'I'll take that money now,' Billy told the bartender.

Word of this incident reached Garrett in Fort Sumner. The ex-cowhand now realized that sooner or later someone would have to stop the Kid. While Billy was far superior to him with a pistol, Garrett was a master of the rifle. He decided he would have as much chance against the Kid as anyone. He saddled up and rode to Lincoln. And it was not long before Garrett was elected Sheriff of Lincoln County, solely for the purpose of destroying the Kid, and through the 'string-pulling' of John Chisum.

His move was not mistaken by Billy. The Kid knew that now their close friendship was at an end and that one of them would have to die.

During the greater part of the year 1880 the Kid and his band roamed the area, rustling cattle and selling them in neighbouring States. The first part of November found the Kid and several of his men stealing cattle from a small ranch near Alamogordo and starting towards White Oaks with them. The Kid sold several to Jim Greathouse. A posse was informed that the Kid and his men had taken refuge at Blake's Saw Mill, near White Oaks. However, the place was found deserted when the officers arrived.

The determined posse, thirteen men under the leadership of Constable T. Longworth and Deputy-Sheriff Bill Hudgens, flushed the Kid and his gang from their camp at Coyote Springs and trailed them to the ranch of Jim Greathouse. On November 27, the posse rode through a heavy snowfall to the Greathouse ranch, where they hemmed in the outlaws.

The posse knew that with guns evened up the Kid probably would come out on top, and Hudgens realized the cost in lives if he attacked the house. It was a dangerous stalemate, both sides afraid to make a move.

Hudgens devised a scheme by which both sides could get out of the spot without taking any chances. They agreed to exchange hostages. Greathouse would go out to the posse's camp and Deputy-Sheriff Carlyle would ride into the ranch premises to surrender to the Kid. Then both sides would retreat from the vicinity and release the prisoners when they were out of range of each other. Actually it was nothing more than the lull before the storm, a sort of guarantee for a talk, as each side probably realized that one would not allow the other to escape.

Unarmed and under a flag of truce, Carlyle boldly rode up to the house and dismounted, then calmly walked into Greathouse's living-room.

However, matters did not set well with Carlyle, who justly

felt that the Kid planned to kill him anyway. He took a desperate chance and dived through a nearby window, but he was not quick enough for the Kid. One shot wounded the officer; a second killed him as he tried to crawl to safety. At the sound of shots Greathouse wheeled his horse into Hudgens' and in the confusion fled back to the safety of his house. Enraged, the men of the posse poured a terrific barrage into the house, but to no avail. The intense cold forced them to withdraw during the night and the Kid with his men escaped. The next day the Greathouse property was put to the torch.

Bitterly disappointed and humiliated by their costly error, the posse returned to Fort Sumner. Later they received word that the brazen Kid was coming back into town to attend a Christmas party, so they summoned Garrett. He rode to Fort Sumner and collected a posse. They hid in a building at the edge of town.

At about midnight five men on horseback came into town. Garrett stepped from the shadows, his rifle at his shoulder, and ordered them all to unfasten their guns and put up their hands. The first rider grabbed for his pistol and Garrett's rifle rang out. The horseman fell out of the saddle, drilled through the chest.

The rest of the riders wheeled their horses and escaped. The Kid, for the first time in his life, had been riding in the rear of the group instead of leading them. The dead man was Tom O'Folliard, one of Billy's staunchest friends and one of the few gunfighters who got out of the McSween house alive.

Garrett was not to be denied after this, and he passed the word that he wanted the Kid, period. Then he started tracking the four remaining riders.

The next day a man named Wilcox sent word to Garrett that the Kid was hiding in an old rock house at Stinking Spring. Garrett and a large posse crept within range of the place and tightened the ring around the house. Then Charlie Bowdre, the only other surviving member of the McSween massacre, stepped out with a bucket.

'Okay, Bowdre,' Garrett shouted. 'This is Garrett. Put 'em up and come this way.'

Charlie tossed the bucket and drew, but when Garrett's rifle thundered he was slammed to his knees, a bullet through his chest. He staggered back into the house with bullets spattering all about him. A moment later he appeared again in the doorway, and to Garrett's surprise he started towards him, revolver in hand. Just exactly what the Kid had said to him nobody knows, but it was Garrett's belief that Billy ordered him to go out and finish the job on the sheriff. He reached his objective too late. As he stepped up to Garrett he toppled dead into the lawman's arms.

'Bowdre's dead, Billy. You haven't got a chance. We don't aim to deal with you like the Murphy boys did. Come on out, and I promise you safety.'

The Kid stepped out, followed by Tom Pickett and Dave Rudabaugh, an escaped convict who had killed a jailer in a Las Vegas riot.

Bowdre's body was thrown into a wagon and Billy the Kid and his two friends were chained together and placed in the same vehicle. Later Bowdre was buried beside O'Folliard.

This occurred four days before Christmas and by December 29 Garrett delivered the Kid and his men in wagons to the jail at Santa Fe. During the trip the two men joked together and seemed in friendly spirits.

'You should have given up when Governor Wallace gave you the chance, Kid,' Garrett told him.

'Hell,' Billy answered, 'if I had I wouldn't be here now.'

'And then you had to kill Carlyle. That will make it all the worse for you.'

'Damn it, Garrett, I did not kill him. His own posse killed him when he went through the window. They must have thought he was me trying to escape. I sent the governor a letter first part of December telling him all about it.'

Rudabaugh's sentence came swiftly. He was automatically sentenced to hang for the murder of the jailer, but when he was returned to Las Vegas he broke jail again and headed for the Mexican border, never to be heard of again.

From the Santa Fe jail the Kid sent letters to Governor Wallace, which went unanswered. At that time William Sherman was United States Marshal at Santa Fe and he permitted no friends to see the Kid, but was all too willing to allow the curious and the morbid sightseers in to see and to heckle the Kid. But that was to be expected. Such was Sherman's nature.

There was a Federal indictment pending against Billy the Kid for his participation in the killing of Buckshot Roberts, but for some reason or other it was thrown out of court. In March 1881 the Kid was taken *via* stagecoach to Mesilla, where he was to stand trial for the murder of Sheriff J. A. Brady. United States Deputy-Marshal Bob Ollinger was the officer who took the Kid to the courtroom each day during the week-long trial.

The Honourable Mr. Fountain was appointed by the Territory to represent the Kid, and although he did his best, he was unable to sway the jury in Billy's favour.

On April 13 the jury found Billy the Kid guilty as charged and Judge Warren H. Bristol sentenced the Kid to be hanged on May 13.

On April 16 the Kid was loaded into an old Army vehicle, handcuffed and with his legs shackled to the back seat. With him went Bob Ollinger, now a deputy-sheriff of Lincoln County, having been appointed on April 15, and technically also still a United States deputy-marshal.

The small adobe jail of Lincoln County was hardly the place to hold such an important prisoner as Billy the Kid. It was decided to place him under guard in one of the stronger buildings—the old Murphy store. Not far off workers were erecting the scaffold upon which the Kid was to die. Throughout the day the sound of hammer and saw drifted up to the second-floor room where the Kid sat waiting, manacled hand and foot, and under constant guard.

One of his guards was Bob Ollinger. He was a mean,

cowardly bully, who tormented the Kid relentlessly. Ollinger was a friend of Beckwith who had been killed at the McSween fight, and at Beckwith's grave he had sworn to have revenge on the Kid.

'Hear that, Kid? That's the trap they're building down there. Couple more weeks and boom! Down you go. Then you'll have a long neck, Kid. Long and broken.'

The Kid sat helpless.

'Why don't you try a break, Kid?' Ollinger continued. 'Try it . . . so we can break your dirty back.'

The taunting went on as the execution day grew nearer. Always the Kid sat quietly, his young face showing no emotion whatever as the insults came from Ollinger.

Pat Garrett had given special instructions to his two deputies, Bob Ollinger and J. W. Bell, to use the utmost precautions in guarding Billy.

'If a mouse hole is left open he'll get through it,' Garrett had told them.

Bell was cautious enough to avoid taunting the gunfighter, but Ollinger persisted in reminding Billy that he was now a prisoner in Murphy's store.

Ollinger was mean and treacherous, through and through. After his death his own mother stated: 'If there is a hell, he is surely there!'

On April 28 Ollinger stepped across the street to eat lunch, leaving Bell and the Kid playing a game of monte in the Murphy upstairs room. The Kid was relaxed and sprawled out in his chair, apparently resigned to his fate. A few minutes after Ollinger had gone, the Kid asked Bell to unlock his leg-shackles and take him to the latrine.

'Well, I don't know,' objected the deputy. 'We'd best wait until Ollinger gets back.'

'He'll be gone for an hour. Come on, Bell, be a good sport.'

'All right. Just a second. I'll get the keys from Garrett's office. You know how careful he is, won't let us have the leg-iron nor the handcuff keys in this room.'

As Bell started to leave the room, the Kid gave his right wrist a peculiar twist and the handcuff dropped off. He leaped after Bell and struck him a blow on the back of the head, then pulled Bell's pistol from its holster. He snapped the hammer back on the weapon and held Bell riveted to the floor, staring into his own six-gun.

'You been okay, Bell,' the Kid said. 'I don't wanta hurt you. Just walk down the stairs easy like and you'll be all right. I want you to unlock the armoury door so I can get some more guns and I'll just lock you in there at the same time. Now be quick about it!'

They started down the stairway to the first floor, a long, winding staircase which curved sharply halfway down. As Bell reached the curve he leaped around the corner and started down the steps two at a time. He took only one step, for the Kid leaped to one side and fired around the corner. His bullet ripped through Bell's heart and smacked into the wall in front of him. The deputy crashed down the steps, dead.

Ollinger was walking back when he heard the shot. He drew his revolver and started across the street on the run. As he approached the store, the Kid's smooth voice stopped him in his tracks.

'Bob! Bob Ollinger!'

He stared up. Billy was looking down from the second-floor window with Ollinger's own shotgun pressed to his shoulders. The big gun roared, and Ollinger twirled from his feet and fell into the dusty street, nine buckshot in his chest.

A moment later the Kid hobbled out on the porch of the store, his hands free, but with legs still manacled. He stood there, staring down bitterly at the dead deputy who had tormented him. The shotgun bellowed again, and the second charge smashed into Ollinger's back.

The Kid then summoned a blacksmith named Goss and at gunpoint told him to split the chain of the leg-irons. The old German was ashen with fear.

'Nothing to worry about, Fritz, but be sure you don't miss with that axe.'

After this had been done the Kid forced a Mexican to saddle a horse, on which he leisurely rode out of town, with no one offering the slightest resistance. Behind him were two dead men. Not another man in Lincoln would have tried to stop the Kid that day. He whistled quietly between his teeth as he rode.

For the next few days Billy rode aimlessly, sticking close to Lincoln and Fort Sumner. His leg-irons were cut off by a friend, José Gorboda, who lived near Lincoln. He spent a few days with Ignacio Salazar, who had been wounded and left for dead in the McSween house battle and who had then drifted back to Fort Sumner.

The Kid had a choice: he could either head across the Border to comparative safety or he could stay in New Mexico. He chose to return to the home of his sweetheart, whose name is lost to record.

Garrett meanwhile was combing the territory with a large posse. His instructions were to kill the Kid on sight. While he scoured every mountain hideaway, checked every bush, and searched from one town to the next, Billy relaxed in Fort Sumner, a stone's throw from the scene of his jailbreak.

Garrett's tip-off came from a tramp and drunkard named George Graham. This village derelict was sleeping in the livery hayloft of the Dedrick stable in White Oak when he overheard Dan and Sam Dedrick, both close friends of the Kid, discussing the manhunt.

'Right under their noses, and them riding all over New Mexico looking for him,' Sam said with a laugh.

Graham understood by this that the Kid was hiding in Fort Sumner. He sneaked from the stable and told Deputy-Sheriff John W. Poe, who did not at first believe him. It seemed too fantastic that the Kid should remain that close.

On the night of July 14 Garrett and two deputies rode into Fort Sumner. They checked first the home of Charlie Bowdre's widow. They were about to leave when Garrett decided to look in on Pete Maxwell, a friend of the Kid's, who lived in a small patio room on the south-east corner of the Bowdre house. Garrett stepped across the porch and entered Maxwell's room. He seated himself near the head of the bed and awoke the sleeping Maxwell.

'Where's Billy, Pete?' he asked.

But before Pete could answer Garrett held up his hand for silence. Outside the room he heard a familiar voice. The chase was coming to its end.

Earlier the Kid had gone up the street to visit Saval Gutierrez, Garrett's brother-in-law. Saval's wife, Celsa, offered to fix him something to eat.

'I'll go on up to Pete's and get some beef,' Billy told her.

The Kid took off his boots and coat and left the house, headed for the Maxwell place, about a hundred feet away. In his hand he carried a butcher's knife and his .41 calibre pistol was hanging at his side.

One deputy sat on the edge of the porch; the other squatted near the fence, while Garrett waited inside. As the Kid walked up to Maxwell's porch he stumbled over the first man, named Poe, and his revolver leaped from its holster.

'*Quién es?*' he snapped.

It was a bright, moonlit night, but Poe did not even recognize the bootless, tousled Kid. Later Poe said he thought the Kid was a frightened sheepherder. At any rate, Poe acted wisely. Had he raised any alarm he and McKinney, the other deputy, probably would have died on the spot, and the Kid would have made good another escape. Instead they jokingly told the youth to calm down.

'We ain't gonna hurt you,' they told him.

But Garrett had heard, and waited—cautioning Maxwell to hold his tongue under threat of instant death. Then the figure of the Kid slid silently into the dark room.

'*Quién son esos hombres afuera*, Pete?' ('Who are those men outside?'), the Kid inquired.

Sheriff Garrett, seated at the head of Maxwell's bed,

levelled his revolver. Even in the dark his action caught the keen eye of the outlaw.

'*Quién es?*' he demanded as he leaped back into the middle of the room, revolver in his left hand.

Two shots roared out in the darkness. One sizzled through a window. Garrett jumped through the open window and flattened himself against the wall, his pistol smoking in his hand. He waited, scared, knowing his second shot had missed by several feet. The Kid would be inside, waiting for a chance to shoot back.

Half an hour crawled by. The three lawmen finally stepped up on the porch, lit a lantern and entered the patio room. Pete Maxwell was waiting for them.

'He's dead,' he said.

The Kid lay in the middle of the floor. In the circle of light from the lantern Garrett saw the telltale hole in his chest. Garrett's first shot had sliced through the heart of Billy the Kid.

The news was slow in travelling. It was not until July 21, eight days after Garrett's bullet had ended the career of Billy the Kid, that the first account of the shooting was published. It was a brief article in the *Cimarron* (New Mexico) *News and Press*:

> . . . We can all unite in the sentiment expressed in the verdict of the coroner's jury that Garrett has earned the gratitude of the whole territory by ridding it of this dangerous outlaw.

Billy's death was accepted as very tragic news in Fort Sumner. The local women, young and old, were deeply grieved, and they tenderly laid the body on a bench with lighted candles around it. They showered flowers over the twenty-one-year-old desperado's body.

The entire populace of Fort Sumner solemnly followed the rickety wagon, drawn by Mexican ponies, to the Kid's last resting-place. Many rumours were persistent that Garrett and his two men had been in danger of lynching by the people, so great was their admiration for the Kid, but nothing substantial has ever been uncovered thoroughly to prove this.

With the announcement of the Kid's death, rumour immediately started that Billy had actually been spared by his friend Garrett. Therefore the news of the Kid's death was greeted throughout the State with doubt. Through the years these rumours grew, and even today people claim the dauntless Kid escaped death. As late as the spring of 1950 one William Henry (Brushy Bill) Roberts came forth with the claim that he was actually Billy the Kid and that he had been living with the Yaqui Indians in Mexico for many years. This same Roberts was a witness to the claims of J. Frank Dalton, who in 1950 tried to prove that he was Jesse James. Both men's stories were eventually discredited.

The Kid's body was identified by an impressive list of friends, and there can be little doubt that he actually died in Pete Maxwell's room that night.

Since no relative claimed the body, the remains of Billy the Kid were laid to rest near those of Tom O'Folliard and Charlie Bowdre, also victims of Sheriff Garrett. A rude cross with 'Billy the Kid' carved into it was erected over the grave, but a group of drunks later used it for target practice and shot it to pieces. For years only a few persons knew the location of the grave, and it is believed now that the exact spot is unknown.

Pat Garrett retired from public life and prospered as a rancher. But, with marked irony, he died at fifty-nine, a victim of treacherous guns in an ambush by business enemies. And old Fort Sumner is now a city of the past. Its buildings have long ago rotted and been blown away by the winds of time. Only weeds and sand-dunes mark the stamping ground and the death place of one of the West's most remarkable gunslingers. A monument to Billy the Kid was eventually erected, after tourists expressed their astonishment that there was none. It stands near the highway, protected from vandals by a fence. It is the only tribute to the last of America's famous gunfighters. Only one other memento remains: in the wall of the old Murphy store in Lincoln, which is now used as a city hall, rests the bullet that killed J. W. Bell.

Although Billy the Kid never crossed paths with Wild Bill Hickok, that famous frontier lawman enters the story and ends it in a curious way. It was Samuel Collins, a wealthy Easterner in Deadwood, South Dakota, for his health, who started that story. Wild Bill Hickok, formerly marshal of Abilene, Kansas, had expressed his contempt for Billy the Kid; and in Deadwood the gold-flush miners and rich merchants would bet on anything. One afternoon Collins bet a miner named Bert Baker five thousand dollars that Hickok would emerge the winner in any duel to the death with Bonney. Baker took him up and they wrote out the terms of the bet and gave it to the bartender in the Criterion Saloon:

> Wild Bill's gun will kill Billy the Kid or Sam Collins will pay Bert Baker five thousand dollars.

A few years after Billy's death—long after Wild Bill had been cut down by the cowardly Jack McCall—Sam Collins was reading an account of the Kid's death, and he stopped cold:

> Pat Garrett was carrying a lucky gun that night he got the Kid. It was the same gun carried by Wild Bill Hickok until his murder and was later given to Garrett by Hickok's sister in Kansas.

Collins had won his bet.

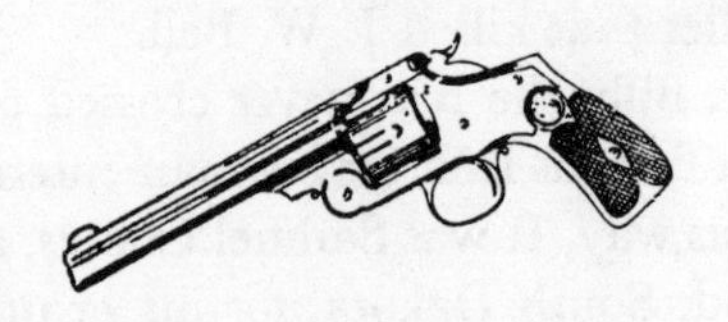

8 Harry Tracy

Of all the Western outlaws, perhaps less is known and less written about Harry Tracy Severns than about any other, yet he was probably the most vicious of the lot. Paradoxically, he was spurred into his life of crime by a love affair which endured infidelity, disgrace, murder, robbery, and imprisonment—a romantic touch to one of the most savage biographies of the West.

Like many other famous Western killers, Harry Tracy—as he was known to law and lawless alike—was not a Westerner by birth, though he fast learned the ways of the young and reckless West. He was born in Pittsville, Wisconsin, in 1875, and taken to Cumberland a few months later. In 1889 his family moved to Minong. The father, Lan Severns, deserted the family, and the mother remarried.

It was in 1895 that Harry headed into the Western Badlands, became a dead shot in a matter of weeks and a cowhand virtually overnight. His contribution to outlaw history provided a fitting end to that violent age. At first he and his younger brother, Irvin, worked on the railroad, but he was discharged.

Harry got into his first serious trouble when he killed a man with his bare fists in a bar-room brawl. At his trial he defeated the murder charge on a self-defence plea. It was at this time, when he left Wisconsin for Chicago, that he cut his name to

Harry Tracy, in order to prevent his family from becoming involved in the disgrace.

In Chicago during his twentieth year Harry Tracy met the charming and innocent young Janet Warrington. They swore an undying love for each other, and she remained true to him until his death. Wanting to make a fortune for her sake, he decided to go to Colorado, the wide-open territory, which seemed to offer every opportunity for prosperity.

In Colorado Tracy discovered he was a fish out of water, for he knew nothing about horsemanship, cattle, or prospecting, the skills required of every man in that raw country. But he was willing to learn, and a natural learner. First he tried prospecting for gold, but soon became disillusioned. Several old-timers advised him to go back to Chicago while he was still young enough to start anew, but he was determined to fulfil his promise to bring back riches to Janet.

When he heard that ranchers in Billings, Montana, were paying well for cowhands—since many cowboys were leaving for the goldfields—he hurried there and applied to an employment agency. When he stated honestly he had very little skill at ranching, but was willing to learn, he was given a chance at a large ranch outside Billings. There everyone was amazed at the way he tackled and learned any job he was asked to do. Even wild horses became docile at his touch, and after practising with a six-gun for a few weeks he was the best shot in the territory—so good, in fact, that somebody accused him of having shammed ignorance of firearms. His marksmanship with a rifle was considered uncanny.

Life at the ranch was pleasant, and Tracy was learning, but he was impatient to get rich and return to his sweetheart. In an effort to increase his earnings he frequented the Billings gambling-rooms, and here he met another cowboy, Sid Phillips, who claimed he had made fast dollars by rustling. When Phillips suggested that they try 'moonlighting', Tracy quickly agreed.

Billings, known as the 'Hole in the Wall' territory, was an area dominated by the deadly Red Sash gang.

'Every cow we steal,' Phillips explained, 'will be blamed on the Red Sash bunch.'

In less than a week as Phillips' assistant Tracy ran off several hundred head of cattle and sold them at a fancy price. He wanted to leave at once for Chicago.

'We can be rich, really rich!' Phillips remonstrated. 'And in no time at all.'

Tracy was hesitant, but one more trip to the gambling-hall convinced him, for at the tables he dropped every cent he had made.

Their second endeavour was not so successful, since Phillips had come under suspicion as a cattle thief and his plan to lay the blame on the Red Sash gang failed because the sheriff set a trap. However, the posse made too much noise as they moved in on the moonlighters, so Tracy and Phillips fled, with the sheriff and his men in hot pursuit. They split up, and Phillips doubled back towards Billings in the hope of throwing them off his track. The sheriff's men, however, were waiting, and he was taken without a fight.

Tracy headed for the upper Missouri River basin, where a canyon served as a natural fortress and could be held indefinitely by one man with enough ammunition. The posse followed, but, being aware of Tracy's skill with a rifle, they were cautious. It was nearly midnight when the faint trickle of pebbles and small rocks gave Tracy warning. He fired one shot down the mountainside and heard a body roll and the other deputies scrambling for cover.

Tracy waited for about an hour, then slipped off his boots and crept down the hillside into his enemy's camp. He picked out the best horse, cut the rest loose, and sent several shots in the direction of the camp before riding off into the night.

Now he was a branded man—but this brush with the Montana authorities opened up vast, lawless fields, and he plunged wildly from one crime to another. He was a lone wolf, rarely trusting anyone to join him after his unfortunate experience with Phillips.

Tracy played the goldfields and cattle ranches for a while, then in 1898 journeyed to Seattle, Washington, which was a young town, still untamed. There he met Dave Merrill, who since his youth had earned his living at petty thievery and who was an escapee from the California penitentiary. They formed an alliance which was to end in tragedy for everyone connected with them.

Their first project was the holdup of a drunk, whose companion they slugged over the head with a revolver. Their take was five hundred dollars, but when they knew the police were close upon their heels they headed back towards the Badlands.

They planned to prey on the gold miners at Cripple Creek, but shortly after their arrival Tracy ran into a former associate from the Billings ranch, who warned him that a deputy from Montana was in the area. This disturbed Merrill, and he suggested they leave at once, but Tracy suggested they hold up a mine worked by two prospectors. While they waited, masked, on the trail for the two men to leave the mine with their diggings, they were amazed to see half a dozen miners emerging from the tunnel. Tracy decided to take on the whole lot.

The miners quickly obeyed the order to 'throw up your hands' when they stared into the muzzles of the weapons brandished by Tracy and Merrill, and these young outlaws netted more than five thousand dollars in gold dust. Then they boldly returned to Cripple Creek and sat in a saloon listening to descriptions of the holdup.

The next morning they boarded a train for Denver, and Tracy, as usual after a job, wanted to return to Chicago in order to see Janet Warrington. But gambling once again proved to be his weakness. Within the week both he and Merrill were without funds. Pressed by necessity, they held up a Denver saloon and locked the patrons in a freezer at the rear, collecting five hundred dollars for the effort.

The series of episodes which led to Tracy's final undoing began in January 1899, when Merrill invited Tracy to visit his home in Portland, Oregan, where his mother and sister Mollie lived modestly in a house at First and Market Streets. Mollie fell headlong in love with her brother's friend. In less than a month the fickle outlaw married the girl, and they moved to a boarding house in Fifth Street which Merrill and Tracy had been using as headquarters. Every evening Tracy would leave the place with 'lunch pail' in hand, to give the neighbours the impression that he was a working man, but once out of sight he joined his partner in terrorizing the city with daring masked holdups.

One of Mollie's former admirers, bitter at having been jilted and suspicious of Tracy's bravado, informed the police that a watch should be put on the Merrill home. The following day Tracy and Merrill were seen there, and a phone call to police headquarters summoned detectives Ford and Cordano and three patrolmen. By the time Cordano and two officers arrived at the rear door and Ford with the other patrolman arrived at the front door, Tracy had left, giving some vague excuse.

At sight of the officers in the front of the house, Mrs. Merrill gave her son the signal. He made a dash for the back, but on seeing Cordano he quickly slammed the door. Cordano and his two companions hesitated, expecting Merrill to open fire on them, and when they rushed in the rooms were empty. Where had Merrill gone? They knew he had not left the house, yet apparently he was not inside. Cordano searched the house foot by foot and finally noticed a large tall-boy in the front room. On a hazy chance he pulled open the over-sized bottom drawer, and Merrill glared out. The thief was curled up in the drawer, unable to fight back, and was taken without a shot having been fired.

Since Tracy had left only moments before the arrival of the police, Merrill and his mother firmly believed that Tracy was the informer who had betrayed the hiding-place. Officers capitalized on these suspicions, and encouraged the confused Merrill to say he expected Tracy to return to the house at First and Market Streets. Detectives Cordano, Ford, and Weiner hid in the house and waited.

Two days went by, however, and Tracy failed to make an appearance. Mrs. Merrill told the officers she expected Tracy at noon on February 6, the next day. The wait continued. Noon came and went. At one o'clock Cordano and Ford left to get lunch, leaving Weiner in charge. A few moments later Mrs. Merrill saw Tracy coming towards the house and warned the detective.

Weiner approached Tracy in the street and presented him with a note signed by Merrill, containing plans for Merrill's escape from prison. Weiner passed himself off as Ben Moore, an ally of Merrill's. Tracy seemed taken in and agreed to accompany Weiner to his hideout.

At Fourth and Market Streets, however, the wily outlaw suddenly yelled and broke for freedom. He dashed across the street to the Union Pacific Railroad tracks and leaped aboard a train which was just pulling out, firing two shots at Weiner as he went. Both bullets missed, but, once aboard the train, Tracy held his pistol against the head of the engine-driver and ordered him to throw open the throttle. The train leaped ahead several hundred yards. Then suddenly the train began to lose speed. The driver hurriedly explained that someone had pulled the emergency cord and there was no way to keep the train from stopping.

Weiner thought he had lost his man, but at sight of Tracy leaping from the cab the brave officer kept running in pursuit, yelling for passers-by to stop Tracy. One citizen, Albert Way, blasted Tracy with a shotgun as he ran past his house, but it was loaded with birdshot instead of buckshot, and the dazed thief kept going. Tracy next cut through a yard to get to Hall Street, one of the main thoroughfares. As he ran into the street he plunged right into Weiner's waiting arms, for the detective had anticipated this move.

This was the first time Tracy was lodged in jail.

Police officers started to work on Tracy, hoping to get him

to sign a full confession of all his crimes, but he stood fast and absolutely refused. Even when police presented him with Merrill's signed confession implicating him in many crimes, he remained tight-lipped and laughed at suggestions that he plead guilty. However, he was tried and convicted, while Merrill entered a plea of guilty.

In the meantime police had been working steadily on Mollie Tracy, hoping she would make a statement to help the prosecution. Although she did not betray her husband or her brother, she was of no comfort to them, for she left Portland shortly after the trial and faded into obscurity.

Tracy and Merrill were awaiting their sentence when Janet Warrington arrived. Even after her lover admitted having married Mollie—strictly as a business arrangement, he insisted—she repeated her pledge of love. She agreed to smuggle guns to Tracy so that he could try to escape. A few days later she managed to deliver a gun to him, and he hid it in his bed.

On the morning of March 21, 1899, an excited crowd packed the Portland courthouse to witness the sentencing of the two outlaws. The jailer, a man named Dougherty, went to the cell to get them.

As Tracy stepped out of his cell he jammed the gun into Dougherty's side and snapped, 'Open all the cell doors or I'll shoot you.'

'Go ahead and shoot,' Dougherty growled back.

The man's sheer courage momentarily staggered Tracy, and suddenly Deputy-Sheriff Jordan appeared in the doorway, pulled his gun, and ordered Tracy to drop his pistol.

Tracy broke and ran down the corridor. Jordan fired two shots at the weaving figure. As Tracy reached the corner he turned to answer the gunfire and accidentally dropped his gun. As he reached the end of the corridor he ran straight into Dougherty, who had sped to cut him off, so he threw up his hands as he looked into the muzzle of the jailer's six-gun.

Tracy was escorted into court and, when the delay was

explained to the judge, he unhesitatingly added five more years to Tracy's sentence. Tracy was taken to Salem Prison, where he began a twenty-year stretch. Merrill was sent to the same prison sentenced to thirteen years.

The law had apparently ended Tracy's reign of terror.

Janet Warrington filled the gap left when Mollie Tracy deserted her killer-husband. She was convinced that Tracy really loved her, and had started on the road to crime only in order to earn enough money to give her the things he thought she deserved. She moved to Salem and got herself a job, visiting the jail whenever possible. But Tracy's only thoughts were of escape. He constantly badgered her to get him new weapons and to assist him in a break. The foolhardy prison officials had placed Merrill and Tracy in the same cell and had put them both to work in the prison foundry. The two men immediately started plans to lead a breakout of all seventy convicts working in the foundry. Once again Tracy's plan failed, this time because an informer described it to the warden.

Several months passed, and the escape incident was forgotten by prison officials. Merrill and Tracy seemed to be model prisoners who had finally learned their lesson. But Tracy had started his third plan of escape shortly after his second failed. He was merely waiting for the officers to relax their vigilance. He knew that two of the prisoners, Harry Wright and Charles Monte, were due for release in 1902, and he prevailed upon them to agree to smuggle guns into the prison foundry by scaling the walls of the prison. He and Merrill were getting impatient with the passing of time. Tracy was sick of working in the foundry all day and lying awake all night trying to evolve a successful escape plan.

Wright was to obtain the money for the undertaking from Janet Warrington. Tracy wrote a letter to Janet which passed the prison censor, for the secret part of the message was written in lemon juice and milk between the lines. Upon his release, Wright went to Janet's home and asked to see the letter. Then he applied a solution of silver nitrate to the paper, and she was amazed to see the message slowly appearing dark brown against the white paper:

My Darling Janet:

It will be a short time before we are together again, but you must help me. The bearer is one of my best friends. Give him three hundred dollars and he will fix things. If you tell anybody, my plans will be upset and I'll have to serve out a long term. Take him to Portland and introduce him to Mrs. Merrill. Tell her she must give him three hundred dollars more and Dave will be free.

Harry

Of course Janet followed the instructions to the letter, and on the night of June 7, 1902, Wright and Monte scaled the prison walls and secreted the rifles and ammunition in the foundry.

The following Monday Merrill and Tracy uncovered the box. They loaded the rifles, strapped cartridge belts around their waists, and filled their pockets with loose bullets.

But before Tracy was to make his break for freedom his viciousness had to be satisfied, for he was nursing an intense hatred. At the time only the wall guards were armed, the guards on the grounds carrying only sticks. Tracy slipped up behind one of them, Frank Ferrell, and shot him in the back of the head.

Tracy and Merrill made their break through the prison yard, dodging from one section to the other while keeping up a running gun battle with the guards stationed on the walls. Two of the sentries toppled from the wall. Tracy and Merrill grabbed a long ladder from the supply room and carried it to the northwest corner of the prison. While Tracy raced up the ladder, Merrill kept the guard engaged with rapid rifle-fire. As Tracy reached the top of the wall he fired point-blank at the man, killing him instantly. Merrill followed his partner up the ladder, and the two men dropped over the wall to freedom.

As they rounded a corner they ran into two guards from the east wall who had been wounded. They were ordered by the escaping outlaws to accompany them as hostages, to prevent the remaining guards from firing on them. When they reached a nearby creek, Tracy shoved his gun near the side of one guard's head and sent a bullet through his brain. The other fell to the ground at the same time and thus miraculously escaped death, for the blood-craving Tracy thought the bullet had killed both men.

Tracy and Merrill easily escaped into Salem, since the blistering gun battle in the prison yard had created mass confusion, and the remaining guards were busy herding the rest of the prisoners back to their cells.

The following night Janet Warrington was in her room reading an account of the escape and its terrible price. Joseph D. Lee, superintendent of the Salem penitentiary, had circulated wanted 'dodgers' throughout the State, offering a reward and giving descriptions of the two outlaws. Janet naturally thought that Tracy was on the move, but at about 9 p.m., when she answered a knock on the door, she was shocked to find him standing there. The two had only a brief moment together, but she gave him a hundred dollars, and he advised her to leave for Chicago at once, since he did not believe the police suspected her part in the escape plot.

Tracy and Merrill now exhibited amazing nerve. They actually walked through the streets of the city in their prison garb until they met a lone man in the street. They attacked him and took his clothes and warned him that if he told the police they would return and kill him. Next they broke into a house and stole more clothes. From there the trail led to stables, where they stole two horses and made their getaway. A neighbour saw them riding off and hurried to the police, who laughed at the story, not believing it possible. Their minds were quickly changed, however, when the theft of the two horses was reported. The police believed the thieves to be Tracy and Merrill.

The following day Sheriff Durbin of Salem addressed a crowd of police officers, deputies, and volunteer lawmen gathered in his office:

'Gentlemen, the men we are dealing with are no ordinary outlaws. In boldness and daring they make Jesse James look like a Sunday-school boy. And in depravity, in out-and-out love of killing, they are worse than any savage that ever lived in our country. There will be a long list of dead and wounded before these two are captured. Every man who seeks them takes his life in his hands. You must be prepared to die. If you are not, you'd better stay at home. They might be in this city at this very moment.'

For the next two months the cold-blooded gunmen held the entire area in a vice-like grip of fear, in spite of one of the most intense and terrifying manhunts.

Tracy and Merrill rode only fifteen miles from Salem before stopping. At the cabin of August King they ate breakfast and paid for the food. King was unaware of the prison break and thought nothing of the affair until he noticed the brand on the two horses tethered to a bush—'LeB,' that of his friend in Salem, Felix LeBranch. As soon as the outlaws departed, King rode off to the general store and by telephone wired Salem. Durbin and Lee arrived swiftly at the head of a posse. Bloodhounds ran the trail to a thick-wooded area, and the lawmen thought they had cornered the killers. It was getting dark, so they surrounded the woods and decided to delay the capture until morning. But Tracy and Merrill had already left the woods and struck out for the town of Gervais.

Dr. C. White and a friend had started for the town in a buggy, on the chance that the two convicts were not in the woods after all. As they entered the town, Tracy and Merrill stepped from the shadows, pistols in hand, took the buggy and rode off, leaving the two possemen standing in an open field close to a deep drainage ditch, in order to avert a surprise attack.

The next morning they returned to King's cabin for breakfast. When King saw them riding up he thought they were coming back to kill him, but they merely wanted to change clothes and eat. For the next few days they circulated freely throughout the area where a mammoth sheriff's posse was combing every inch of territory.

'Keep quiet about this,' Tracy told King. 'We'll be back in about a month.'

No coward, King immediately hurried to Gervais and warned the lawmen, who rushed back to the King cabin, certain they would capture the convicts this time. They might have been successful, but, as the sheriff approached from one side, the two outlaws worked their way into a deep gully which ran through a field near the King place.

Tracy and Merrill split up temporarily. Tracy stole a horse and rode back into Salem to see Janet Warrington, only to find that she had followed his suggestion and left for Chicago.

Tracy and Merrill met by appointment at Needy and headed for Clackamas County, a wild and mountainous section which was sure to thwart the posse, and, besides, Clackamas was out of Durbin's jurisdiction. Durbin gave up the search at the county line, and other members became discouraged also. The terrain was so rough that even the National Guard abandoned the hunt.

After remaining in hiding for almost a week Tracy and Merrill stole a team of horses and a wagon from a farmer near Oregon City, and drove to East Portland, passing right through the centre of town without arousing the slightest attention. They abandoned the wagon near East Portland and set out on foot for the Columbia slough, where they forced two men to row them across into the State of Washington, promising to send them fifty dollars for their trouble. As soon as the bandits disappeared among the trees, the owners of the boat contacted the authorities in Salem by telephone. Durbin then called the sheriff of Clark County, Washington, warning him that Tracy and Merrill were now probably on their way to their former address in Seattle.

Sheriff Marsh of Clark County was a shrewd police officer, and he calculated that the two would attempt to reach the dense woods north of the river. With nearly two hundred men, he guarded every possible approach to the woods and also staked out guards along a road which ran between the river and the trees. That night Tracy and Merrill sneaked across the road within earshot of the guards and entered the thick woods.

About three miles from the town of Orchard lived an elderly man named Henry Tiede. Early that morning he had been awakened by a loud knock on the door, and, upon opening it, he had found himself face to face with Tracy. The old man was not alarmed.

'Good morning, Mr. Tracy,' he said. 'Come in and have something to eat.'

He explained that he recognized him and Merrill from newspaper pictures and sat quietly while they ate. After helping themselves to fresh clothes, they tied the old man up and threw him on the bed. He begged them to cut him free, explaining that since he lived alone he might starve to death. Tracy shrugged as he and Merrill left. Tiede rolled off the bed a moment after they were gone and sawed his ropes off against a sharp edge on the stove. Then he rode to Orchard and gave the alarm.

Once again the law had a trail to follow, but once again the dogs could not find the scent and the chase was abandoned.

While several members of the posse made their way to Vancouver, Washington, Bert Biesecker and Luther Davidson went to the bridge near Vancouver Pike to stand guard.

At about midnight Davidson spotted two men stooping over the water's edge near the bridge, drinking. Biesecker and he took careful aim and fired. One of the shots geysered into the water inches from the head of one of the bandits. Merrill and Tracy ran quickly for cover, and they circled and crossed the river behind the two guards. They found the officers' buggy and drove it several hundred yards up the road, then parked it again and slipped into the woods. When the lawmen discovered their buggy had been moved, they began a cat-and-mouse game with Tracy and Merrill.

An hour passed. Biesecker and Davidson believed the

criminals had taken flight, so they decided to go home. As they walked up to their buggy Tracy and Merrill opened fire from the woods. The two deputies jumped into the buggy and, stretched out on the floor, thrashed the horses into action while bullets ripped through the sides and whined over their heads.

The next morning Biesecker and Davidson returned to the scene of their narrow escape and, with the aid of bloodhounds, picked up the trail once again. It led to the town of Ridgefield, where the posse learned that the outlaws had robbed a farmer of two horses and his money. The dogs, hot on the scent, ran on towards Lewisville, and from there to La Center. Sheriff March believed they were only an hour behind the fleeing killers, when suddenly the dogs began to yelp and run off in all directions. The scent seemed suddenly to have ended. March discovered that Tracy had sprinkled his trail with red pepper, so the dogs were lost, and the posse returned to Vancouver.

Tracy and Merrill next took on the identity of deputy-sheriffs and twice stopped at farmhouses for food after explaining that they were part of the posse searching for the outlaws. In both cases the farmers recognized them. One of the farmers rode immediately to town to warn Sheriff Totten of Skamania County that Tracy and Merrill were in the area. While Totten and his men were speeding, the bold escapees showed up at another farm and bought their supper, once again identifying themselves as members of the posse.

Sheriff Marsh summoned a third posse from Cowlitz County, believing that Tracy and Merrill were now firmly hemmed in. But a week went by and neither posse nor dogs found a trace of the killers.

The next break came when William Taft, a rancher at Castle Rock, in Cowlitz County, informed the posse that the two men had used one of his line shacks for shelter. He returned with several well-armed citizens, but their prey had once again escaped.

During their desperate flight, Tracy and Merrill time and time again acted with paradoxical strategy. Once they stole two horses from the ranch of Joseph Alberti, and a few moments later they stopped a man to ask directions to Silver Lake. The man was Alberti, who recognized his horses and asked where they had got them. Tracy told him they had purchased them from a man further back on the road, but he turned the animals back to Alberti and continued on foot. It seems strange that in the desperation of escaping a posse these two cold-blooded killers would calmly turn over two stolen horses to their owner without a fight. Tracy was completely unpredictable, and probably this was one reason the posses scouring the entire area were having such a difficult time running him down.

Tracy now was beginning to realize that two men stood less chance of continuing to escape the growing party of lawmen and citizens, so apparently he decided to dispose of Merrill. This incident was pieced together from people who claimed that Tracy told them the story.

On the night of June 30 the two men were seated at a campfire when suddenly Tracy said: 'Dave, seems to me you might be getting ready to run off and desert me.'

Merrill looked surprised.

'That ain't true, Harry. I thought maybe it was smart to part company back in Oregon when the heat was really on us. But you wanted to stick together, so it's okay with me.'

'I think you'd lead me into a trap if you had the chance.'

'What's the matter, you trying to start a fight?'

'Not with the likes of you. Wouldn't be worth it.'

Tracy neatly led Merrill into a word battle, and before he was through it was apparent that only one would leave the place alive. Finally Tracy suggested they settle the argument with a duel.

'We'll stand back to back. I'll count ten and then we turn and fire,' Tracy said.

Merrill had little choice. He also was a crack shot, probably deadlier with a pistol than Tracy. But he should have realized that the ruthless Tracy would never put the duel on an even basis.

TRACY SEEN NEAR SPOKANE

Spent a Day at a Ranch West of That City

HE HAS THREE HORSES

Took Fresh Animals and Enforced Complete Secrecy

HE THREATENED TO RETURN AND DO SOME KILLING IF HIS PRESENCE WAS MADE KNOWN—HE TALLIED WITH THE DESCRIPTION SENT OUT.

SPOKANE, Wash., July 31.—A Wenatchee special, to the Spokesman-Review, says:

From 10 o'clock yesterday morning until 9 at night, Harry Tracy was an unwelcome guest at the ranch of W. A Sanders and S. J. McEldowney, six miles down the Columbia river. Tracy had three horses. He carried a Winchester and two revolvers. Toward evening he forced McEldowney to bring him two fresh horses. He then took Sanders' saddle and left. He threatened that if his presence were made known he would return and do some killing. He tallied exactly with Tracy's description, even to the mole on his face.

At Ellensburg.

ELLENSBURG, Wash., July 31.—Sim Evans, living fifteen miles north of Ellensburg, reports to Sheriff Brown that on Monday a man calling himself Tracy demanded food at the point of a gun. The stranger had a wound on the head. He inquired the way to the Columbia river, and warned Evans not to give him away. The sheriff thinks Evans was imposed upon by a man impersonating Tracy.

BATTLE WITH HARRY TRACY

Noted Oregon Outlaw Surrounded by Officers

IN SWAMP NEAR CRESTON

A Long-Range Rifle Fire Exchanged With the Posse

REINFORCEMENTS SENT TO THE SCENE FROM ALL DIRECTIONS, AND SEVERAL SHERIFFS ARE CO-OPERATING IN AN EFFORT TO CAPTURE THE FUGITIVE.

SPOKANE, Wash., Aug. 5.—Harry Tracy is surrounded in a swamp near the Eddy farm, eleven miles southeast of Creston, Wash. For four hours before the special messenger left for reinforcements, a long range rifle fire between Tracy and the posse of eight men headed by Sheriff Gardner, had been in progress. The news was brought to Creston by Jack McGinnis, a member of Sheriff Gardner's posse. A telephone message from Davenport at 12:40 a. m. states that McGinnis reached there shortly before midnight. Twenty-five armed have left in wagons for the scene of the battle. Sheriff Doust, of Spokane county, is leaving at the time of filing this message. In his party are eignt or ten armed men. Another wagon load of man hunters will leave at 2 o'clock tonight, and more will go as soon as daylight breaks. Sheriff Cudihee, of King county, is guarding the Sprague road, while Sheriff Deboit is on the road leading to Edwall.

Law officers close in on Harry Tracy in the swamps near Spokane, Washington

The strange duel between the two hunted killers began. The men stood back to back and started to pace off as Tracy's voice droned out:

'One . . . two . . . three . . . four . . . five . . . six . . . seven. . . .'

On the count of seven Tracy wheeled and fired. Merrill's head jerked forward as the bullet crashed through the back of his skull, and he plunged to the ground. Tracy rolled him over with his foot, held the gun at arm's length, and fired another shot through his forehead.

A letter was sent by Harry Tracy to his mother. It was dated July 15, 1902, and postmarked Spokane, Washington. The letter bore no inside address, and the envelope was addressed simply to 'Mrs. Edwin Riley Goodvin, Minong, Wisconsin'. Goodvin was the name of Mrs. Severns' second husband. The letter ran:

DEAR MOTHER:

Just a few lines about Merrill. Don't believe what the paper says about the so-called duel. I made that up so that law would not have the satisfaction of knowing they had wounded Dave and he died a couple days after. Dave was dead as he'll ever be when I shot him in the back of the head and then made up the duel story to account for it. There's a lot of stuff printed about us that we don't know nothing about. If I don't see you again in this world then I will in the next. Good-bye.

Your son,
HARRY

If this letter contains the truth, then all the accounts of the duel are in error. However, Tracy certainly was vicious enough to carry out the plan. Tracy's mother made no effort to use the letter to vindicate her son in the matter of the duel. It has not been published before, and was not known to exist until recently. Perhaps Tracy's mother knew better than to believe him.

Two days later Tracy attacked and bound an elderly

farmer, Daniel Laird, and ate food at his farmhouse. After he left Laird succeeded in breaking his bonds and rushed to Belmore to summon the posse. Word was spread to Olympia, and several of the officers concentrated the search on Castle Rock, where Merrill had relatives. The law still did not know that Dave Merrill was dead.

Tracy rode through Olympia at midnight and stopped at the warehouse of the Capital City Oyster Company. Entering a cabin he held two men at gunpoint with a repeating rifle and ordered them to fix him something to eat. A few minutes later two others entered and were ordered to sit down and keep their hands in view.

Tracy next summoned Captain Clark, owner of a launch near the oyster company's docks, and the man arrived at the wharf with his son. Tracy ordered him into the boat. The captain at first refused, but when Tracy identified himself he changed his mind. Tracy bound and gagged two men and ordered the other four aboard the boat.

'If you try anything I'll kill you,' he said. 'I've killed a lot of men—two or three more won't matter.'

He ordered Clark to head the launch towards Seattle. Later the captain described the trip as the worst experience in his career. He said Tracy seemed irrational and insane at times and once ordered Clark to pull close to McNiel's Island so that he could take a few shots at the guards. The captain convinced him it was not a good idea. During the trip, Tracy bragged about the killing of Merrill, but claimed that his one-time partner had turned on the count of five, fired at him, and missed.

At 6 p.m. they arrived in Seattle, and Tracy ordered them to take the boat several miles down-river to Meadow Point. He bound the four men and ordered Clark's son to accompany him. They walked up the rail tracks to Ballard, just outside Seattle, and Tracy told Scott Clark where he had left Merrill's body. The boy did not believe him and did not investigate.

At Ballard Tracy left Scott, telling him he was going on into Seattle. The lad rushed back to the launch and released his father and the other men, who hurried to Seattle to spread the exciting news. The hunt was on again.

Men swarmed over the Seattle area, searching for the desperate outlaw, guessing that Tracy was hiding in Bothell, a suburb. In a gully at the edge of town footprints led to a nearby cabin.

As the lawmen were about to leave the gully a rifle-shot rent the air, and the bullet grazed a deputy's head, knocking him down. A second shot rang out and the bullet thudded into another deputy's body. He toppled back into the ditch, dead.

The others started to lay a new plan to trap the killer, but a few minutes later three shots rang out in quick succession, and one of them staggered into the clearing with three bullet-holes in his body.

The lawmen then withdrew, for Tracy had killed one and wounded three of them.

Tracy's brutal gun battle at Bothell called into the bitter fight one of the most relentless lawmen in the West, Sheriff John Cudihee. Cudihee set up a guard-post system, ordering every man to remain at his specified post no matter what news reached him.

'The only way to capture him,' Cudihee said, 'is to wear him out. Run him till he drops.'

The system worked. Tracy was on the run. He raced from Bothell to Ravenna, stole a horse from Perry Vincent, dashed to the farm of Lewis Johnson and ordered him to hitch up a team and wagon and drive him towards Freemont. There he stopped briefly at the home of Mrs. R. H. Van Horn to get something to eat. While he was there with Johnson, a grocer's boy came to the house and Mrs. Van Horn slipped the youngster a note to warn officers in Freemont that Tracy was in her home.

There were two police officers in the town. They summoned an insurance agent, and began the journey to the Van Horn residence. *En route* they met Sheriff Cudihee in company with a handful of men who were also on Tracy's trail. In the meantime a neighbour of Mrs. Van Horn's looked in at the house, and Tracy forced him to remain inside. When he prepared to leave the house he told Johnson to get on one side of him and the visitor on the other side. Naturally, neither the sheriff nor his men expected to see three men leave the house. The Freemont lawmen came up to them and asked what had happened to Tracy, and Tracy replied, 'He left half an hour ago.' Both the law officers, however, knew that nobody had left the house in the past hour. One stepped back and drew his gun.

'Throw up your hands, Tracy!' he cried.

Tracy stepped behind Johnson, drew quickly and sent a shot crashing through the lawman's head, killing him at once. The other drew, and, instead of shooting at the outlaw, ordered him to drop his gun. Once again Tracy's gun roared, this time blasting the other in the chest. He died shortly afterwards. Tracy dashed into the woods, with the sheriff and his men emptying their guns at his retreating figure.

Tracy once again confounded the officers, for instead of heading for some remote part of the woods, he backtracked to the Van Horn home and followed the main road back to the city.

He spent one night at the home of Bud Brettman, a former Salem Prison convict, who warned the outlaw that the house was being watched. It was a ruse to get rid of Tracy, but he paid no attention. He preferred to enjoy the soft climate of the city. He went to bed and slept soundly until nearly midnight.

It was July 4, almost a month after Tracy's daring escape from Salem Prison. After leaving Brettman's house he spent the night in a cemetery, where he had hidden his rifle, and then calmly walked about the city, watching the people as they went about their various celebrations for July 4. Tracy spent part of the day roaming about the docks, getting a big thrill from watching the various big ocean-going vessels docked there. There was some shooting of fireworks and firecrackers, but rather on a mild scale, he thought.

The next morning he went to the home of August Fisher, ate and helped himself to clothes, and left the Fishers tied up.

It took them several hours to untie their bonds, but they did not inform the sheriff of their meeting with Tracy because he had warned them he would return and kill them all if they did.

By now the entire city was under surveillance. A twenty-four-hour guard had been placed on all roads leading in and out. Yet that night Tracy returned to the home of Brettman. This time he merely gave Brettman a message to deliver to Janet Warrington in Chicago. He left at about midnight and travelled to the city limits in a tram car. He spent the night asleep in the woods at Meadow Point, where the Clark launch had taken him days before.

The next morning he rowed out to a small fishing boat and ordered the man to take him to Bainbridge Island, near Port Madison, about fifteen miles from Seattle. It was late at night when he alighted from the boat, so he slept in the grass again. The next morning he entered the home of John Johnson and forced him to prepare a meal. He left the Johnson family tied and forced a hired man named Anderson to accompany him. Before leaving he asked the Johnsons the direction to Port Gamble; when they freed themselves they informed Sheriff Cudihee that they believed he was heading for that place. Tracy had, of course, taken Anderson off in the opposite direction.

During the next few days he was seen with Anderson by several people. Two women and a boy talked to him while they were picking berries, and a man named Gerrells rushed to the police after Tracy entered his home and ordered him to go to town and buy two revolvers, threatening to kill Anderson and the entire family if he warned the police. The police rushed to Gerrells' home in Renton by special train, but Tracy heard the train approaching and warned the women to act with care. The police surrounded the house and Anderson, whom Tracy had tied and left on the back porch, managed to work the rope loose and ran into the barn.

This time Tracy actually crept across the yard while police were watching the house and walked through the cordon. He sprinkled the trail once again with pepper, and when his escape was finally detected, the sneezing dogs abandoned the chase.

Once during these days an expert rifle-shot named Fisk actually had Tracy in his sights when the outlaw was riding past the house, but Mrs. Fisk asked her husband not to shoot, fearing Tracy might be someone else. Tracy next hid out at the home of E. M. Johnson, and this time dispatched Johnson into the town of Kent, several miles away, to buy him a pair of revolvers. He gave Johnson three dollars and warned him that if he was not back by 6 p.m., or if he told the sheriff, his whole family would be killed. Johnson returned with one revolver and two hundred cartridges, and Tracy left on one of his horses. The horse, however, soon returned, and it was evident that Tracy had ridden only a few miles and then released it. The next day Johnson told Cudihee about Tracy's visit.

While Cudihee and his men concentrated on scouring the woods near Kent and Auburn, Tracy brazenly walked down the rail tracks in full view. Once Deputy-Sheriff J. A. Bunce and his son saw him and demanded that he halt. The outlaw made for the woods, and the sheriff and his son fired several shots at him. As he ran, Tracy encountered another deputy and fired a quick shot at him. The bullet grazed the man's scalp, but did not seriously injure him. Once again the convict had escaped almost as if by magic, but this time Sheriff Cudihee assured his men that Tracy's days at large were numbered. He told them that Tracy was walking into a trap which nature had prepared for him.

The trap was a sprawling swamp, miles wide, with insurmountable cliffs on both sides. It was so treacherous that Cudihee believed Tracy could not possibly get through it, and it was into this swamp that Tracy had gone. But Tracy quickly realized the danger and reversed himself, rushing back to the edge of the mire.

Several times during the next five miles Tracy backtracked, then went forward again. The dogs plunged into the swamp, then turned and raced back after him. His circling tactics threw the animals off, and they were soon hopelessly engulfed in the series of trails he had left.

In the meantime the outlaw had gone to a farm and demanded a horse. Both of the farmer's animals were too old to ride, so Tracy went into the house and had him prepare something to eat. While he was there a wagonload of deputies passed the house without stopping. They were on their way to the swamp, believing that Tracy was still floundering around.

For days Tracy wandered about the countryside. He stopped at farm after farm, demanding food, clothing, shelter. Once he walked into a home when a young man was shaving and demanded that the boy shave him. The frightened youngster actually had a razor at Tracy's throat but never scratched him, he was so frightened. The family did not report the incident for two days. Tracy on another occasion forced an elderly man to sit in a shed for several hours and just talk, because, the outlaw explained, 'I'm tired and need a little relaxation.'

The newspapers were following the hunt with fevered anticipation. Each day articles gave the latest developments. On Friday, August 1, 1900, the *Daily Oregon Statesman* reported:

Spokane, Wash., July 31—From ten o'clock yesterday morning until nine at night, Harry Tracy was an unwelcome guest at the ranch of W. A. Saunders and S. J. McEldowney, six miles down the Columbia River. Tracy had three horses. He carried a Winchester and two revolvers. Towards evening he forced McEldowney to bring him two fresh horses. He then took Saunders' saddle and left. He threatened that if his presence were made known he would return and do some killing. He tallied exactly with Tracy's description, even to the mole on his face.

North Yakima, Wash., July 31—The shoes worn by Harry Tracy are on exhibition at a prominent business house in this city. They were captured by a posse of deputy manhunters on the Wenas Creek, about twenty-two miles east of this city. Tracy could not be found. He had stolen all the valuables from a sheepherder's cabin and departed. When seen by a boy, he said he was Tracy, and he was leaving the country. He asked the distances and direction to Roza, on the Northern Pacific Railroad, and took up the trail for that station.

A report that Tracy was in Yakima County was circulated about the city from a man who appeared much excited, and anxiously inquired for the sheriff. He had seen and talked with Tracy. The bandit had robbed his cabin and exchanged shoes. . . .

An armed posse immediately set out for Roza to apprehend the bandit. After a long, hard ride they found the little cabin. . . . His trail showed he had gone towards the railroad, but he could not be found. The men returned, very much disgusted, one of the posse remarking that 'the man who led us there is one of the biggest liars in Yakima County'. But the shoes are on exhibition and attract much attention.

Tracy managed to work his way back to Eastern Washington, and the sheriffs of all these counties quickly united in their efforts to track him down. Cudihee, not to be denied the opportunity of capturing the man who in his county alone had killed three officers and wounded several others, rushed east and joined the search. Tracy, however, was becoming more and more wary and was no longer creating so much of a show. It was not until August 5 that a farmer named Dakin, near Odessa, found the following note tacked on his well:

Thanks for the cool drink. The finders of this note will please send word to Sheriff Cudihee that he had better get back to his own territory. I will fix him if he keeps on bothering me.

HARRY TRACY

Apparently the note had been left there two days earlier, for on August 3 Tracy had held George E. Goldfinch and the entire Eddy family at gunpoint nearly the whole night. The next morning he released Goldfinch with a stern warning to go straight home and keep silent. The boy returned home, fully resolved to tell the sheriff that the outlaw was at the Eddy farm. However, Tracy's warning preyed so heavily on his mind that he waited until the following day to ride into nearby Creston and telephone Sheriff Davenport.

This telephone conversation was overheard by J. J. Morrison, a railroad man, who formed a posse and raced to the place and found Eddy working in a field.

'Where's Tracy?' they demanded.

The farmer was too terrified to admit that Tracy was still there. For two days the family had been held in a grip of terror, afraid to move for fear of being shot. Now, even with aid at hand, the farmer was still petrified, and he said that Tracy was gone. But just as he said it, the outlaw walked out of the barn and started towards the house. The posse closed in, and Eddy was sent back to the house. When he entered Tracy was waiting.

'Who were the men in the field?' he demanded.

'Strangers,' the terrified Eddy answered. 'I never seen them before.'

'Come with me,' Tracy ordered.

The two men left the house and sauntered out to the barn. Then suddenly Tracy broke, rushed into the building, and grabbed his rifle and cartridges, and made a dash for a nearby gully. A volley from the posse stopped him short, and he dived behind a hayloft. Rifle bullets ripped through the hay around him and he rolled over, got to his feet, and ran behind a large boulder. As he did so, a rifle bullet ripped through his leg.

The wounded outlaw plunged into the wheat and crawled seventy-five yards on his hands and knees while the five men closed in on him. They found the trail of blood and doggedly followed it. Tracy meanwhile secured himself behind a high rock from which he could command the entire field, and he pinned the hunters down with a wilting fire from his high-powered 30-30 rifle. But the battle was a stalemate, for Tracy was confined in his new hiding-place. Every time he moved he

He Warns Cudihee.

SPOKANE, Wash., Aug. 5.—"To Whom It May Concern: Tell Mr. Cudihee to take a tumble and let me alone, or I will fix him plenty. I will be on my way to Wyoming. If your horses was any good would swap with you. Thanks for a cool drink.

"HARRY TRACY."

Such was the note found this morning by C. V. Drason, a phominent farmer living about a mile north of Odessa. The note was pinned to the well where he waters his horses. His farm is not far from that of Mrs. Craben, who saw a mysterious man with two horses passing by her house Sunday night. The scene of the great chase is slowly shifting toward the east. Apparently the outlaw is in no hurry, having tatken five days to cover a distance which a well-mounted man might have traveled in 21 hours.

The officers apparently are working on the theory that he is trying to reach the Rock Lake country, in Northern Whitman county. Three deputy sheriffs from Sprague started in to the Colville Lake country this morning to investigate a rumor that two horses much like Tracy's had been seen by train hands. Sheriff Doust, of Spokane, and a posse were working in that region last night, while Sheriff Gardner was supposed to be working south and west of Harrington. Up to noon no one who has seen the convict has been heard form.

Harry Tracy, as he killed and looted his way across Washington and Oregon, often left sarcastic notes of this type marking his trail exposed himself to a deadly barrage from his pursuers. As dusk descended a shot ripped through his arm.

Tracy knew that the game was up. His leg was broken, so he could no longer run. His arm was shattered, making fighting impossible. Defeated, he turned his famous Colt .45 against his temple and blew his brains out.

The stalemated lawmen, however, did not realize that Tracy had killed himself. Afraid to move, they waited throughout the long night. Cudihee arrived with several other officers, and the field and an adjacent swamp were surrounded. Guards were placed on every road, and men were staked out all over the field, waiting for dawn. When the sun came up one of the men spotted the dead convict. He lay on his back behind the rock, one stiffened hand still caressing his trusted 30-calibre repeating rifle.

Cudihee was called over to identify the body. He looked down at the remains of Harry Tracy and nodded quietly.

'It is a fitting end.'

Thus the long, long trail of bloodshed which had begun with a lover's kiss years before in Illinois ended dismally at the edge of a Washington swamp.

The body was taken to Davenport, while headlines screamed: HARRY TRACY RUN TO EARTH AT LAST.

Hundreds milled around when the train arrived with the bandit's body in Davenport that afternoon. Clothing was torn from it by curiosity seekers, while others pulled locks of hair from his head. Following an inquest, the body was taken back to Salem Prison, and there buried beside the remains of Dave Merrill.

Tracy, like Plummer and Reno and Burrow, who had become outlaws for selfish gain and who had killed recklessly, was vicious, relentless, and cold-blooded. There was little of the glamour about him which folklore has attached to Billy the Kid, the Daltons, Sam Bass, or the James brothers. He lived and died savagely, in final tribute to the American West which was once the thieves' Paradise.

And, like most men who took to the wrong side of the law, Tracy left behind at least one broken heart. Several months after his death the last note he had written to Janet Warrington was delivered. A voice from the grave, it was a final pledge of his undying love.

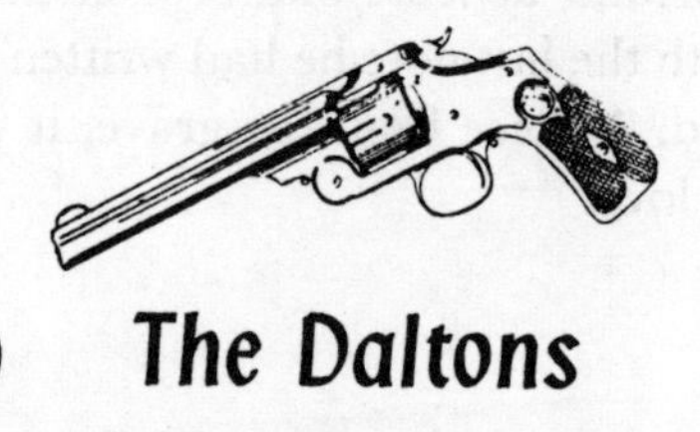

9 The Daltons and Billy Doolin

On April 22, 1889, a pistol-shot was fired that echoed throughout the South-west, for it was the signal that the fertile lands of the vast Oklahoma Territory were open to a screaming, racing, land-hungry line of ten thousand immigrants. It was from this land rush that the infamous Dalton gang grew.

Unlike the James boys or the Bass gang or even Rube Burrow, the Daltons were hated by the law and citizenry alike. Vicious, bloodthirsty, and daring, they carved a name for themselves in the history of Oklahoma. Their careers ended where they had begun, at Coffeyville, Kansas, on October 5, 1892, in one of the most sanguine gun battles ever fought in the streets of an American town.

In 1888 the Daltons had moved from Indian Territory to a farm near that Kansas town, to await the opening of Oklahoma. There were ten sons, five daughters, and a niece. The Daltons had once been prosperous, respected Southern plantation owners, but the Civil War had wiped out their fortune. Now the parents, Louis Dalton and Adeline Younger Dalton—half-sister of Colonel Henry Younger, who fathered the famous Younger brothers—lived in the past, a surly, rude pair constantly talking of their lost wealth.

The Dalton carnival of crime revolved around four of the brothers: Emmett, eighteen at the time of the Oklahoma rush; Grattan, twenty-five; Robert, twenty-one; and William, twenty-three. Not much is known about the rest of the family except that Frank earned an honest living attached to the Arkansas office of the United States deputy-marshal; Ben was a successful Coffeyville farmer; and one daughter married a prosperous farmer named Whipple in Kingfisher, Oklahoma.

The year prior to the land rush Bob had fallen in love with Minnie Johnson, his cousin, and his love was returned. But the young girl became lonesome when Bob and Emmett rode off to Arkansas to serve in the marshal's office with Frank, and soon she was eyeing Charles Montgomery, a handsome young man employed by Theodore Seymour, whose farm adjoined the Daltons'.

When Bob returned he was puzzled by Minnie's coolness until his father apprised him of Montgomery's courtship. The girl warned Montgomery, and the two fled to Coffeyville and boarded the train to Kansas City. The embittered Bob emptied his rifle at the passing train, shooting out several windows and frightening the passengers, but Montgomery and his young fiancée escaped.

The train-shooting episode was quickly forgotten, for Kansas was raw country then, and the mere shooting at a train was hardly enough to cause any concern to the law. Bob, however, felt that Montgomery would be back, so he waited. During the winter Montgomery did return to the Seymour ranch, to gather up the belongings he had left behind. Bob Dalton followed him as he rode back towards town and shot him through the neck. Montgomery was dead when he hit the ground.

Had Bob shot the man face to face there would probably have been no question raised, but many of the Daltons' closest friends doubted the young marshal's story that he had shot Montgomery in the act of stealing horses. The records were stamped according to this claim, however, and Bob actually was paid by the Fort Smith, Arkansas, marshal's office for shooting his enemy in cold blood.

It was several weeks later that the territory was opened to settlers at a cost of one dollar five cents an acre, first come, first served. The land rush was a rough-and-tumble business. Robbery, murder, and brawling flourished, and many honest settlers were either forced off their claims at gunpoint or shot to death. In some instances persons with legal rights to be in the territory first laid claims to choice pieces of land, but these claims were later contested and the settlers were forced to relinquish their rights.

The monumental task of establishing law and order was entrusted to the United States marshal's office and his men. At the time these fearless deputies roamed the territory and maintained law it was difficult indeed to secure efficient men to take the trail against nefarious outlaws at a salary of two dollars a day.

The record reveals that Grat and Emmett Dalton were both assigned to the Fort Smith (Arkansas) marshal's office, first under United States Marshal Carroll, then under United States Marshal Jacob Yoes. However, because of the low rate of pay at the law-enforcing end, Bob Dalton drifted into several 'outside money' deals with land-grabbers. It was while visiting the camp of one of these law-breakers that Deputy Ransom Payne discovered the connection, and the three Dalton brothers were forced to flee.

From that day on the Daltons were hunted men, and their careers of bloodshed and banditry spread.

Their father had carved out a fine strip in the newly acquired territory near Kingfisher, which was becoming a thriving town, but he missed Coffeyville and finally returned. The three brothers knew that the Kingfisher strip would be closely watched and that their Coffeyville home would also be under surveillance, so they kept on the move. Bob was barely twenty-one, the toughest of the three. An expert horseman who seemed to sleep with one eye open, he had a reputation for being a quiet man who never drank to excess and a deadly shot with a lightning draw. He became the strict and demanding leader of the trio.

Throughout the winter months of 1889 the Daltons

plundered with savage delight, using an old Quantrill tactic of dispersing after each raid and then reassembling after things quietened down. It was during one of these cool-off periods that Grat Dalton was captured while examining the barns of a wealthy farmer. Grat was taken to Fort Smith jail, where he felt sure his brothers would rescue him, but Bob here manifested his shrewdness. He waited until the grand jury held its investigation. The jury returned a 'no bill', and Grat was released for lack of evidence. Shortly afterwards the three brothers decided to go west in search of new and fatter targets.

Thousands of persons travelled the Southern Pacific Railroad line from Los Angeles to San Francisco every week, seeking relaxation at winter resorts or in the mountains north of San Francisco. The line carried a lot of money, and its officials bragged that it had never been held up by any desperado. This was true primarily because almost the entire trip was through thickly populated areas—all save one short section.

After leaving Tulare the train had to crawl up into the mountains a short distance and then cross to Kern County, also heavily populated. The crack Atlantic Express left San Francisco at nine each morning, scheduled to arrive in Los Angeles the following morning at about eight. In the short strip between the slow crawl up the mountains and populous Kern County lay the village of Alila, and the train never stopped there unless it was flagged down.

On the morning of February 6, 1890, the train chugged lazily up the mountainside, the passengers drowsing and a quiet game of poker in progress in the drawing-room coach. As the train reached Alila it slowed. A few of the passengers gazed out of the window, but nobody thought too much about the unscheduled stop.

Then half a dozen shots roared out and someone screamed, 'It's a holdup!'

A few minutes before the arrival of the train at Alila five armed and masked men had ridden into the town on splendid horses and had taken over the depot. One of them had flagged down the train and, when the engine-driver stepped out on his platform to find out why, two of the other men swung into the cab with revolvers drawn. A steady volley of rifle-fire kept passengers and train crew in the coaches. The masked man ordered the fireman to accompany him to the express car. When the messenger refused to open it, the robbers smashed the door with picks. The fireman whirled as they went through the door, apparently attempting to escape, and one of the bandits opened fire. He toppled off the platform, dead. The messenger fled to another car, and the outlaws were faced with an impregnable safe. They attempted to shatter the steel door with crowbars, but were unsuccessful, and finally had to flee empty-handed.

The engine-driver and express messenger placed the fireman's body in the express car, then raced the train to the next station, where the news of the holdup and murder was telegraphed to the headquarters of the Southern Pacific Railroad. William Smith, the railroad's chief detective, and several carloads of men, horses, and guns left Los Angeles for Alila, and within eight hours after the holdup a determined band of lawmen was on the trail of the outlaws.

Luck was with the posse, for Grat Dalton's horse had stumbled and a large gash had been ripped open in Grat's side. The trail of blood led to the home of a prominent politician—William Dalton, in Tulare.

Grat and Bill Dalton were immediately arrested, but Bill was able to prove he had been nowhere near the scene of the holdup. He was freed, thanks to the support from political friends, who felt it was only natural Bill should have opened his door to an injured brother.

Grat did not fare so well, however. He was identified by his voice. Both the engine-driver and the messenger claimed he had stood guard in the cab while the other outlaws broke down the express-car door and shot the fireman to death. This fact prevented his conviction on a murder charge, but he was sentenced to twenty years in the State Penitentiary for complicity in the robbery attempt.

$5,000.00

REWARD

FOR CAPTURE

DEAD OR ALIVE

OF

BILL DOOLIN

NOTORIOUS ROBBER OF TRAINS AND BANKS

ABOUT 6 FOOT 2 INCHES TALL, LT. BROWN HAIR,
DANGEROUS, ALWAYS HEAVILY ARMED.

IMMEDIATELY CONTACT THE
U.S. MARSHAL'S OFFICE, GUTHRIE, OKLAHOMA TER.

This typical reward poster describes Bill Doolin, a notorious follower of the Daltons before he became leader of his own gang

On April 1, 1891, Grat began his long trip on the daylight train to the State Prison, hobbled at the legs with a tight thong and handcuffed to two deputies, one by each arm. Once they were safely aboard the train, one of the officers left Grat in the company of the other and went to the smoking-car. Between Fresno and Berenda, as the train crossed a trestle bridge over a stream which ran adjacent to the tracks, Grat suddenly leaped up, jerking the bewildered officer off the cushions. Before the guard could gather his senses the handcuffs were dropped off by means of some Houdini-like trick that to this day remains unexplained. Grat dived through the open window into the swiftly moving water. The guard was too dazed even to pull the emergency cord. The conductor jerked it and the train pulled to an abrupt stop. The guards searched the stream's edge in vain. All they found were the hoofprints of two horses.

Bob Dalton realized California was the wrong spot for the operation of the gang. Their train robbery had been a failure, and only Grat's incredible escape had spared him a long term in the State Prison. So Bob decided to return to Kansas and Oklahoma, where the terrain was known.

However, they had inaugurated their system on the California train, and it became their trademark at every one of their jobs afterwards. They always forced the door of the express car by having the fireman call out to the clerk, they never robbed the passengers, and they always fired a volley of rifle bullets at the train in departing.

In an age when the telegraph was in widespread use, it seemed incredible that the Daltons could roam freely, molesting and robbing at will. Many people became afraid to send valuables through the mails or to travel by train. Heavy rewards were posted for the gang, and William Smith, chief of the detective staff of the Southern Pacific Railroad, personally took charge of the search. Smith was a shrewd man. He anticipated Bob Dalton's return to Oklahoma.

Smith was aware that he would need the assistance of the officers in Oklahoma and, on his arrival in Guthrie, contacted the noted Heck Thomas, Burl Cocks, Ransom Payne, and an Indian named Tiger Jack, who was a deputy-marshal with expert knowledge of the area and uncanny skill in tracking men. It was not too long before Tiger Jack picked up the trail of the Daltons, and a bitter chase began.

For seventy-two hours the Daltons held the lead, and finally the trail-weary officers stopped to eat at the entrance to a canyon on the Cimarron River. Tiger Jack, after a bite, trod off to check the canyon and soon returned waving his arms frantically. Payne and the other three officers joined him, crawling up the side of the canyon. Below them, waiting to ambush them, were the three brothers. Tiger Jack had scented their horses. His keen sense of smell was an asset which was to save the posse many times in the future.

The anxious officers decided to make a flank attack, but they took too long in circling, and when they reached the spot their prey was gone. The pursuit dragged on through three more days, but the posse had lost the Daltons. Exhausted, the lawmen returned, and Smith went back to California.

Payne vowed to chase the Daltons every time they were spotted, and he ordered a watch placed on the Dalton home and the Whipple ranch owned by the Daltons' brother-in-law. A rancher, Fred Carter, rode into Kingfisher one day and, seeing a sorrel tied to the Whipple rack, went straight to the marshal's office and reported that the horse was his and had been stolen several days earlier. Ransom Payne urged Carter to prefer charges against Whipple. Whipple was arrested and placed in the United States Penitentiary to await trial. As Payne had hoped, Mrs. Whipple immediately contacted Bob Dalton, then took a train to Wichita, to be near her husband during his trial.

On receiving the message from his sister, Bob Dalton decided to loose the vengeance of the Dalton clan on the town of Kingfisher, and also to hold up the train carrying Whipple to prison. He sent a skull and crossbones signed in blood to the mayor of Kingfisher, warning him that he would rue the insult to the Daltons. Before any of their plans could be carried out, Bob learned that Carter had refused to prosecute Whipple and that his brother-in-law had been released. This changed Bob's plan for jumping the train. While in the Red Rock Creek hideout, he learned that Payne was going to return to Guthrie aboard the Santa Fe-Texas Express, which passed through the town of Wharton in the Cherokee Strip.

They rode to Wharton, donned masks, held up the station agent and cut out the telegraph wires. One of the bandits took a red lantern and flagged down the train. Payne, who had a berth in the last coach, summed up the situation as the train slowed to a stop. He looked out of the window and saw the masked men swinging aboard. Quickly he slipped off the rear of the train and hid in the bushes along the right-of-way. Frustrated in their attempt to kill Payne, the Daltons smashed into the express car in routine fashion and got away with almost two thousand dollars. As they rode off they passed within a few feet of the hidden Payne, who quickly ran back to the station, spliced the telegraph wires, and sent a message. But the Daltons had vanished.

United States Marshal Grimes realized he had a tough problem on his hands, so he sent for his most able men: Payne, Kress, Joe Jennings, and Ed Short.

Bob, Em, and Charlie Bryant, a Dalton new recruit, were in need of a suitable hideout. Charlie's sister Daisy had become infatuated with Bob Dalton, and he persuaded her to go to the town of Hennessey, in Kingfisher County, to buy a frame house for them. The three men and their 'moll' then settled down. Payne soon received word of this and took several men to investigate. Unfortunately Bob and Em left a few days before the lawmen arrived, leaving Daisy Bryant with her brother, who was drunk and unable to travel. Payne and his men rushed the house and captured Bryant and the woman, but were disappointed in not getting the Dalton boys.

On August 23 Ed Short took Charlie Bryant aboard the train for Guthrie. During the trip Bryant was taken back to the messenger car, and there Short asked the messenger to keep an eye on him while he looked over the train. The messenger thought Bryant looked harmless enough, manacled as he was, and laid his revolver aside for a moment. Bryant jumped up, grabbed the revolver, and dashed for the door. Just as he did so Short stepped through the express-car door. Bryant shot him through the chest. The gasping Short toppled over, reaching for his revolver as he fell. With his last ounce of strength he levelled down on the fleeing bandit and fired one shot. The bullet ripped through Bryant's spine, and he crashed over to the train platform, dead. A moment later Short too expired.

Bob and Em realized that, with the death of the respected Ed Short, the law would never rest until they were caught. They disappeared into Indian country, and months went by without a sign of them. Meanwhile Daisy Bryant was released from Guthrie Prison, and Payne placed her under surveillance, guessing that Bob would return to her sooner or later. She opened up a dress-shop and settled down, but one night she too disappeared. Marshal Grimes issued a statement to the effect that the Daltons had been driven from the territory for good.

But Bob Dalton was planning a robbery by which he hoped to match the James and Younger brothers. Deep inside the Indian country, supplied with food and shelter by friendly redmen, he and Em and two additions to the gang, Tom Evans and a man known as Texas Jack, were preparing their greatest holdup. Throughout the autumn and winter these four men and one woman made their intricate plans.

On June 2, 1892, they struck. Their target was the Texas Express, the same train they had held up the night Payne narrowly escaped death. They picked the small town of Red Rock in the Cherokee Strip for the daring holdup. They were six now, for Grat Dalton had returned from California to cast his lot again with his brothers, and still another recruit supplemented the band.

The train pulled into Red Rock at 9.40 p.m. The depot

was taken over, the wires cut. As the driver hauled the train to a stop, the six bandits leaped aboard. The bandits collected two thousand dollars.

Payne rode to Red Rock and trailed the outlaws into Greer County. The futile chase, which lasted for ten days, was described in the *Stillwater* (Oklahoma) *Gazette*, June 10, 1892:

On June 4, Sheriff John W. Hixson of Logan County returned from the trail of the Red Rock train robbers. When he left the pursuers of the robbers they were sixty miles west of Red Rock. There were twenty-five deputies in the party and he said they would press on until the trail ended or the robbers were overtaken. United States Marshals Payne and Madsen were in the Panhandle country at that date with a posse of men watching to prevent their escape. The two posses are now pursuing a northerly course through the Strip. A party has started from Caldwell, Kansas, going south, in sufficient numbers and fully armed, to do good battle in case they intercept the fleeing road agents. It seems, beyond doubt now, that the robbers are none other than the Daltons and their colleagues, as has been generally believed since the robbery. The latest reports are that the robbers were on the trail leading to Fort Supply and their pursuers were following them very close. A posse had started from Fort Supply to intercept them. A hard-fought battle may be expected at any time. It is to be hoped that this band of ruffians may receive a lesson that will deter others from attempting to follow their example.

It is known that five brothers of this now notorious family of criminals are in this territory along with an aged mother. The mother lives near Kingfisher, on a claim. Some days ago Bill, the oldest of the boys, returned to his mother from California, where he has recently been acquitted of the charge of train robbery in that section. Bob and Emmett are also wanted by the Golden State authorities for holding up a passenger train there some years ago, and their guilt is positively known. Grattan, or 'Grat', as he is known among his pals, is an all-around cattle and horse thief and robber of stagecoaches. With the exception of Charley, who lives near Kingfisher, the family of sons are known to have committed every crime from imposing upon younger schoolmates at school up to robbing their defenceless fellow-men after they became older. . . .

On July 15 Bob and his gang struck again. That night eight well-armed, well-mounted masked men rode boldly into the tiny hamlet of Adair, followed by a wagon. They came slowly, tying their horses in front of the depot.

The *Stillwater Gazette* on July 22, 1892, gave a graphic account of what followed.

Parsons, Kans., July 16—The coolest and most desperate train robbery ever perpetrated on the Missouri, Kansas, and Texas Railroad took place at Adair Station on the Cherokee division of the road about nine-thirty o'clock last night, resulting in the killing of one man, the wounding of three others and the loss to the express company of a large sum.

The notorious Dalton gang, who had been camped in the Indian Territory, between Adair and Prior Creek, for several days, made their way to Adair about nine o'clock last night and at the muzzles of Winchesters, pointed in the face of the station agent, ransacked the office of the station of all its money and valuables. Having accomplished this the robbers, seven in number, sat down at the station and coolly awaited the arrival of passenger train No. 2, due there at nine-forty-two o'clock.

When the train was slowing up at the station the robbers covered Engineer Glen Ewing and his fireman with their Winchesters and no sooner had Conductor George W. Scales and his porter stepped off the train than both of them were also forced to face Winchesters.

Three of the robbers then compelled the fireman to leave the engine and with his coal-pick aid them in securing admission to the express car. Up to this time Messenger George P. Williams had persisted in his refusal to open the door. One of the bandits then shouted that he had placed dynamite under the car and would blow it to atoms if the door was not opened. He fired, by way of emphasis, several shots into the car, which passed uncomfortably near the head of the messenger and he gave in and opened the door. . . .

While the three robbers were in the express car, a fourth was seen to back a spring wagon to the door of the car and the contents of the safe were thrown into the wagon.

When the train stopped at Adair, Capt. J. J. Kinney, chief of the detective force in the Missouri, Kansas, and Texas, Capt.

Leflore, chief of the Indian Police, and seven other guards were in the smoking-car of the train, expressly to protect the train from any attack from robbers. The robbers, the moment the train stopped, began firing their Winchesters and kept the firing up until they had accomplished their aims. Kinney and his men opened fire on the robbers and for a few minutes bullets were flying thick and fast. . . .

When the train reached here Express Messenger Williams had not fully recovered from his experiences and in a talk with a reporter, stated that he did not know how he opened the safe, as he was ignorant of the combination and that if he had to do it over again he could not do so to save his life. . . .

Vigilante Committees began to spring up throughout Kansas, Oklahoma Territory, and Indian Territory; and an impressive reward was offered by the Pacific Express Company for the arrest and conviction of the bandits—five thousand dollars for each, with a limit of forty thousand for all; an enormous sum in those days.

Demands were made upon the Government to do something about the Daltons. It was unanimously agreed to put Ransom Payne at the head of a vast pursuit party charged with the responsibility of tracking them down. Other obstacles would have to be hurdled as well. For all holdups were not being committed by the Daltons alone. The successful Dalton raids, however, encouraged other bands of outlaws to spring into existence and every crime committed was charged to the Dalton boys.

One particularly daring raid imputed to the Daltons occurred in July 1892, when a band of masked men descended upon the town of El Reno. No one but the wife of the president was in the bank building when the outlaws entered and demanded all the cash. The outlaws robbed the bank of over ten thousand dollars in cash, so serious a loss that it was forced out of business. Who were the perpetrators? No one knows.

While Payne and his party were gathering in the Oklahoma

Territory, Em, Bob, Grat, and Daisy Bryant met in the Fort Smith, Arkansas, underworld for a family reunion. Bob was now planning their greatest job—the robbery of not one, but two banks in their home town of Coffeyville, Kansas. It was with this double bank robbery that he hoped to eclipse the reputations established by Jesse and Frank James and the Younger brothers. The banks were the C. M. Condon and Company Bank and the Coffeyville First National. It was the first time anyone had ever attempted to take two banks simultaneously, and Bob was impressed with his plan.

Emmett hotly protested, reminding Bob that their father and brother Frank were both buried there. Em also felt that the people of Coffeyville had been decent to them, but Bob turned a deaf ear. The robbery was on.

They met Dick Broadwell and Bill Powers and planned the holdups. Bill Doolin, generally conceded to be one of the shrewdest holdup artists who ever lived, was with them when they started, but he turned back, pretending his horse had thrown a shoe. Doolin felt the Daltons were headed for their Waterloo.

The double event was set for Wednesday, October 5, 1892. The evening before the men rode into Onion Creek Bottoms, near the Davis farm, and camped for the night. Amos Burton, a Negro cowboy, was left out in the Cherokee Strip with a covered wagon, to await the return of the loot-laden outlaws. He waited three days, then went into Hennessey, where he learned of the Dalton disaster.

The bandits turned into Maple Street and rode past the Long-Bell Company and down to an alley which ran between Maple and Walnut Streets. In this alley several teams were tied at the rear of Davis's blacksmith shop, and opposite the McKenna and Adamson stables stood an oil-wagon owned by the Consolidated Company. Bob ordered his men to dismount in the alley and to tie their horses to a fence bordering the property of Judge Munn. Bob, Grat, and Dick Broadwell donned false black beards, but Emmett didn't trouble to follow their example. Bill Powers's own thick moustache was a partial disguise in itself.

They walked towards Walnut Street directly across from the Condon Bank and slightly to the east of the First National, Grat, Bill Powers, and Broadwell in front, Bob and Em behind. Alec McKenna was on the steps of his store, watching the street through disinterested eyes. Suddenly he grew alert—for he recognized Bob Dalton despite the heavy beard. He quickly retired to his store in fear. The first three robbers walked across the street and entered the Condon Bank, while the other two hurried up the street to the First National.

As they disappeared into the banks the cry rang out: 'Robbers in the banks! The Daltons! The Daltons!' for McKenna had given the alarm.

In front of the First National, Cyrus Lee sat on an ice-wagon. He also recognized the bandits. At first people laughed when they heard the shouts, but Lee set up the same cry, and the street was suddenly alive with running people. Many of them dashed into the hardware stores seeking arms and ammunition.

Bob and Em quickly covered the clerk and cashier, as well as several customers. Bob demanded every cent in the bank, and the clerk started piling the money on the counter. Em found the vault open and tossed nearly two thousand dollars into a sack, forcing the book-keeper to assist him. The bandits forced the three bank employees in front of them as hostages, and started out of the door.

The square before the building burst with gunfire. Bullets crashed through the bank windows and whined angrily off the walls. The hostages fell to the ground and Bob and Em retreated into the bank with bullets ripping around them. They ran through the rear door and out of the bank, still carrying the sack of money.

In the Condon Bank Grat, Powers, and Broadwell were not so lucky. The cashier used his head. It was nine-forty-two, and he knew that the vault door was closed, but not locked. He took a chance and told Grat the time lock was set to go off at nine-forty-five and that the vault contained eighteen thousand dollars. The ruse worked: Grat said he would wait. It was these three minutes that cost four of the bandits their lives.

While they were waiting, Grat ordered the cashier to stuff all available money into a paper bag. The owner of the bank, who lived upstairs, rushed down with a pistol in hand, but took one look at the Winchesters and retired to his rooms. Outside, a harness-maker named Miller fired a shot through the window of the bank, and it tore through Broadwell's arm. It was then that Grat heard Bob's gun bark three times in succession, the signal to leave. Yelling at the top of their lungs, the three outlaws dashed from the bank, into a hail of bullets. They ran along the side of the bank with lead chewing the walls around them as they headed for the alley, their guns roaring answers to the gunplay of the townspeople.

Bob and Em had by now made their exit from the First National and had run directly into Lucius Baldwin, who attempted to block their way. Bob turned the Winchester on him, squeezed off one shot, and killed him instantly. He and Em ran towards their horses, and, as they passed a chemist shop, he spotted two men he knew, Charles Brown and George Cubine, both old and respected citizens of Coffeyville. He killed them both. The First National's cashier had run to a store and grabbed a rifle. He dashed back and dropped to one knee, aiming at Bob Dalton. Before he could pull the trigger, Bob whirled on him and sent a shot crashing into his face, inflicting a serious wound, but not a fatal one.

Bob and Em were joined at the alley by Grat, Powers, and Broadwell. But before they could even mount their ponies a volley poured into the alley, followed by a second and a third. Powers's horse reared and plunged dead. Bob Dalton's jerked and fell to its knees, legs thrashing, and then rolled over. Marshal Charles T. Connelly rushed towards the alley, his gun blazing, and Grat dropped him dead in his tracks.

Kloehr, a livery-stable keeper and crack shot, ran south along Ninth Street until he came to the rear of his stables, then crept up behind the fence to which the gang had hitched their horses. Running through the barn, he got to within five feet of where the determined outlaws were making their bullet-riddled stand. Kloehr peered over the fence and saw Bob ejecting a cartridge out of his gun. Instantly Bob was aware of Kloehr's presence and he turned on his heel, working a new cartridge into the chamber. Before he could pull the trigger, Kloehr shot him in the stomach. The bandit chief bounced backwards, sat down in the street, and rolled over dead. Grat saw his brother drop and quickly raised his rifle towards Kloehr, but again Kloehr was quick. His bullet ripped through Grat's neck. The second Dalton spun around and fell dead in the street.

Emmett, shocked at the sight of his two dead brothers, grabbed the money sack and made a run for the west end of the alley. Bill Powers swung into Grat's saddle, stiffened, and plunged face first into the dust, a bullet in his heart. Broadwell, already astride his mount, whipped it and started out of the alley, but raced straight into a deadly volley. He bounced out of the saddle and rolled over into Maple Street, dead.

Only Em was left. He turned then and performed an act of heroism which would probably have earned him a medal in any other kind of battle. He rushed back to the side of the dead Bob and, standing in a hail of bullets, tried to lift his dead brother's body on to his horse. A bullet ripped through his right arm, and he tried again with his left. Another bullet tore through that and he tried to drag himself into the saddle. From nearby a barber dropped him with a shotgun blast in both legs. Emmett rolled over in the street, critically wounded.

Gunsmoke drifted lazily across the streets of Coffeyville. At the mouth of the alley, the five bandits sprawled, four of them dead. Four of the town's citizens also lay dead. The street was littered with dead horses.

To Kloehr went the credit for turning the tide of battle, for he had killed three of the badmen—Bob, Grat, and Powers—and shortly afterwards he was awarded a gold medal by a group of Chicagoans who wanted to encourage law enforcement.

People crowded around Grat's dead body and raised and lowered the arms, to see a spurt of black blood gush from the hole in his throat. They snipped off locks of Bob's hair. Photographs were taken of the dead men as they lay beside the fence where they had fallen. Some of the townspeople even held up the dead bodies to have pictures of themselves snapped in the act. The authorities wanted to bury the bodies immediately to prevent the public from mutilating them, but they were not buried until the following day. The two Daltons were refused burial in the family plot, and had to be interred in the Potter's Field on the outskirts of town. The four bodies were placed in black varnished coffins, and two graves were dug a short distance from the grave of Charles Montgomery, Bob Dalton's first victim. In one of these graves Bob and Grat Dalton were lowered, while in the other the coffins of Powers and Dick Broadwell were placed. The following Saturday two men arrived from Hutchinson, Kansas—George Broadwell, a brother of Dick, and a Mr. Wilcox, a brother-in-law. They received permission to rebury Dick in a new suit and an expensive coffin, but no inquiries at all were made regarding Bill Powers, *alias* Tom Evans.

After the fight Emmett Dalton was carried to a hotel called the Farmer's Home, where he was treated for his wounds, and at first claimed his name was Charley McLaughlin. But it was no use, since too many folks in Coffeyville knew all the Dalton boys. At first there was open talk of lynching the wounded bandit. The next morning Emmett identified the four dead outlaws. A doctor told the crowd that Em had, at best, only several more hours to live. He wanted to amputate Emmett's arm, but the young bandit refused to allow it. As days went by, Emmett Dalton continued to improve.

Several days after the Coffeyville shooting, John Kloehr received the following letter:

Arkansas City, Kansas

DEAR SIR,

I take the time to tell you and the people of Coffeyville that all of the gang ain't dead yet by a damn sight and don't you forget it. I would have given all I ever made to have been there the 5th. There are five of the gang left, and we shall come and see you all some day. That day, Oct. 5, we were down in the Chicasaw Nation and we did not know it was coming off so soon. We thought it was to be Nov. 5. We shall have revenge for your killing of Bob and Grat and the rest of them. You people had no cause to take arms against the gang. The bankers will not help the widows of the men that got killed here, and you thought you were playing hell when you killed three of us, but your time will soon come, when you'll have to go into the grave and pass in your checks for the killing of Bob and Joe Evans and Texas Jack, so take warning. We will leave you in the hands of God for the time.

Yours truly,
THE DALTON GANG
and Sympathizers of the Gang

This threat was not carried out. For a while it was rumoured that Bill or Ben Dalton was planning to swoop down with a large band, and an official dispatch to this effect was once sent to Coffeyville from a Wells Fargo detective. Precautions were taken, but the citizens were not molested.

As Emmett Dalton continued to improve, Ransom Payne advised him to make a full confession of the Coffeyville affair. Em agreed, and Bill Dalton, meanwhile, rushed from California at the news that his family had virtually been wiped out. This final blow ruined for ever any hope he had of continuing in politics, and actually resulted in his own life of crime.

On October 11 Em was moved to the Independence, Kansas, jail by Sheriff Callahan of Montgomery County.

FRIDAY. :: OCTOBER 7, 1892

EIGHT PAGES.

DALTONS!

The Robber Gang Meet Their Waterloo in Coffevville.

LITERALLY WIPED OUT

A Desperate Attempt to Rob Two Banks

FOUR BAD ROBBERS KILLED

The Fifth One Wounded and Captured.

These triumphant newspaper headlines of October 7, 1892, announce the end of the Dalton gang in Coffeyville, Kansas

He remained there for five months, then appeared before Judge J. D. McCue. He was charged with the shooting of George Cubine and Lucius Baldwin, in addition to bank robbery. His attorney, Joseph Fritch, advised Emmett Dalton to plead guilty, for he felt reasonably certain that he could thus get a lighter sentence. Emmett did plead guilty, and was sentenced to life imprisonment in the Kansas State Penitentiary at Lansing. Capital punishment was prohibited in Kansas at that time.

And so Emmett Dalton, cowboy, officer, and outlaw, began his life within the grey walls overlooking the Missouri River. There he became a model prisoner and learned expertly to tailor men's clothes.

One time Emmett was asked what happened to the forty thousand dollars reward that was offered for the Dalton gang, and he stated that only about two thousand was paid.

In 1907 Emmett was pardoned by Governor E. W. Hoch, after having served over fourteen years in the prison. After his release Emmett married the ever-faithful Julia Johnson at Bartlesville, Oklahoma. They later moved to Hollywood, California, where Em became a building contractor. He died on July 13, 1937.

The real tragedy of the family was the ruin of Bill Dalton. At the time of the Coffeyville battle, Bill was a respected and honoured member of the California Legislature. Although he had successfully overcome the stigma caused when Grat staggered into his home the night of the attempted robbery of the Southern Pacific Railroad, this final blow left him no choice but to resign. He returned to Oklahoma, a bitter and downcast man.

Appalled by the viciousness of the townspeople, he even threatened to sue the city for having allowed his brothers' bodies to be mutilated. But the Press merely made fun of his ire.

Ironically, Bill Doolin, 'Bitter Creek' George Newcombe,

alias Slaughter's Kid, and Charlie Pierce had been ruled out of the Dalton gang because they were not smart enough. Bob always referred to Doolin as the valiant clown. Yet they were free, and the Daltons all but annihilated.

After leaving Coffeyville Bill Dalton sought out Bill Doolin and told him he wanted to join his band. The wise Doolin, however, at first did not want to take Bill into his gang on account of the other Daltons who had been led to destruction by the reckless Bob Dalton.

'Bill,' said Dalton, 'there's nothing left for me any more. I am a social outcast on account of my brothers and I can never return to California. I feel I have a justifiable anger at the society which is treating me this way for something over which I had no control.'

Doolin realized that Dalton was older than his brothers, more settled, and was a man of courage and good judgment. He decided to take Bill into his gang and it was a wise choice. Doolin, Dalton, Newcombe, and Pierce formed the nucleus of the new outlaw band. It was one of the most effective gangs of outlaws then operating in Oklahoma and adjacent States. While most other bands were comprised of ordinary thugs and killers, the Doolin bunch was a shrewd group of mén, most of whom had entered criminal careers through motives of revenge similiar to those of Bill Dalton. Doolin himself was a man of unusual perception and judgment. He had once held an important job in the management of the famous Oscar Halsell's ranch in Oklahoma. But he was not content with that sort of life and began to organize his band in the early 1890's.

One of the first robberies committed by the organized Doolin gang was the holdup of the Spearville, Oklahoma, bank in 1893.

Their next raid occurred several months after the Spearville affair. This time the bank at Southwest City, Missouri, was robbed. It was here that Bill Dalton killed his first man. One of the auditors had tried to fire a pistol at him, so Bill quickly cut him down with a .45 slug. On their way to the Territory they stopped off at Pawnee, Oklahoma, and relieved the bank there of about ten thousand dollars. Business was good.

It now became a deadly game of hide and seek as the redoubtable Bill Tilghman, Heck Thomas, and other noted law officers took after the outlaws as they flitted from one bank to another. But Doolin was clever. He managed to throw off pursuit so effectively that the officers knew nothing of the band's whereabouts until after they had struck another daring blow.

But the fight at Ingalls, Oklahoma, on September 1, 1893, was the beginning of the end. The Ingalls fight indeed is one of the red periods in outlaw history.

The outlaws and an innocent bystander became involved in the Ingalls battle with five officers. Other deputies arrived later, but the nucleus of the group entered the little prairie town on the Cimarron River in a covered wagon. It was high noon at the time.

Across the street from the little bar-room lodging called the Pierce Hotel, the officers saw the outlaws' horses tied in front of the livery stable. Dalton, Doolin, Newcombe, and Pierce were in the bar. Half a dozen cowboys and farmers also lounged about in the noonday heat. Upstairs, sick, lay Arkansas Tom Jones.

From the shelter of the covered wagon the five officers opened the fight with a surprise volley fired into the saloon. Bystanders quickly ducked for cover. The outlaws sent a hot return of lead in the direction of the wagon. Within a few minutes three of the officers lay dead. The remaining two managed to slip away and did not return.

Arkansas Tom Jones—otherwise Roy Daugherty—was forced to surrender, and was placed in the Payne County jail. Although he contended he had not fired a shot in the Ingalls fight, he was unable to substantiate his non-participation in the affray and was sentenced to a fifty-year term for manslaughter.

On May 21, 1894, Roy Daugherty was taken to the Territorial Prison, Lansing, Kansas, to begin that sentence. In 1908 he was transferred to the Oklahoma State Penitentiary at McAlester, and paroled on November 26, 1910, through the efforts of his brothers. He seemed to have reformed, but in 1917 he was involved in the holdup of the bank at Neosho, Missouri. Captured and sentenced to serve eight years in the Missouri State Prison at Jefferson City, he was discharged on November 11, 1921. Not long afterwards he was accused of complicity in the Asbury, Missouri, bank holdup and became a fugitive. On August 6, 1924, when he resisted arrest at Joplin, Missouri, police officers shot and killed him.

The Ingalls battle created quite a sensation through a rumour that a beautiful young girl called 'Rose of the Cimarron' was instrumental in the escape of Bitter Creek Newcombe, her supposed sweetheart, and that she had run the gauntlet of gunfire to bring him ammunition. Who was this fabulous girl whose name has been kept a secret for so many years? From the known facts, it seems that Rose was not even there that day. Arkansas Tom, in an eye-witness account of the fight, makes no mention of Rose of the Cimarron.

Many accounts have claimed that Rose was arrested and sent to the Women's Prison in Massachusetts so that she would be unable to render further assistance to the Doolin bunch. The records of the Department of Correction, Massachusetts Correctional Institution, Framingham, fail to indicate the admission of any Rose Dunn in the entire year of 1896.

There is no record of Rose ever being arrested.

Rose's maiden name was Dunn, and she was born September 5, 1878. She earned the title of Rose of the Cimarron not because she rode with noted outlaws or because of the Ingalls legend, but simply because she was a superb horsewoman and a good friend of many persons living along the banks of the Cimarron.

Several years ago, poor Rose died, still haunted by the ever-growing legends which had started at Ingalls. Rose was a modest girl, and the legends woven about her name during her youth had caused her to seek a seclusion which lasted most of her life.

The two Bills were neither sadists nor swashbucklers. They talked over operations like business men, one advising the other. They condoned no rashness or unnecessary violence where their men were concerned. The characters of these two men can be summed up in an incident which occurred after the holdup of the Rock Island train near Dover, Oklahoma.

A posse from the town was quick to take up the outlaws' trail. In a running battle Red Buck Waightman's horse was shot from under him. Red Buck escaped with the rest of the Doolin bunch by riding double with Bitter Creek Newcombe.

As the outlaws passed an old farmhouse Red Buck called to Newcombe to pull up, so that he could get himself a horse from the corral. Red Buck jumped the fence, and was about to ride off on a horse when the owner, an old preacher, tottered from the house and called to him. Without hesitation Red Buck shot and killed the old man.

'Damn you, Red Buck!' Doolin cried. 'That was not necessary.'

With the posse pursuing them he pulled his pistol and commanded Waightman to dismount. Doolin then conferred with Dalton for a few seconds and they decided to drive Red Buck out of the gang. The money from the holdup was divided then and there. Doolin tossed Red Buck his share.

'Now get, damn your hide. You're not fittin' to be associated with a decent bunch of robbers!'

Red Buck met his just end on October 2, 1895, when he was killed by officers in a hideout near Arapaho, Oklahoma.

As silently as ghosts the Doolin-Dalton gang carried out its precision robberies. Shortly after the Dover affair the gang rode quietly into Woodward, Oklahoma, and went to the home of the express agent. At gunpoint they took him to his office. There they forced him to open the safe containing six thousand five hundred dollars. No one knew about the robbery until the next day, when townspeople found the poor agent tied up in his own office.

July 1895 found Pierce and Newcombe hiding out at the Dunn ranch, but luck was against them. Two ranchers recognized them and a gunfight ensued. When the smoke cleared Pierce and Newcombe were dead.

The Doolin-Dalton gang broke up in 1895, but there was to be no peace for the two Bills as lawmen kept up a constant search for the one-time members of the gang. Most of the outlaws had been accounted for. Only Dick West and the two Bills remained at large.

To locate Dalton the officers had trailed his wife. She had been under constant surveillance for some time. In September an Indian scout who followed her from Ardmore, Oklahoma, to her home twenty-five miles away, spotted Bill Dalton working on the farm. Deputies were immediately summoned and they surrounded the place. On September 25 Dalton walked out of the house towards the shed. He was ordered to surrender. Beaten, broken-hearted, his career ruined, his family dead, and his own soul stained by the same acts he had deplored in his brothers, Bill Dalton calmly reached for his gun and was shot dead by Deputy-Marshal Loss Hart.

Perhaps the most ironic finishing touch to the history of the Daltons and Bill Doolin occurred in mid-July 1896. Officers had been tracking the wily Doolin for months, and he was finally located at his home near Lawton, Oklahoma. It is generally believed that he was shot to death by United States Marshal Heck Thomas. Actually, however, Mrs. Doolin walked out to greet the officers as they rode up. She quietly told them that Doolin, who had been suffering from consumption for years, had died in his sleep. Thomas entered the room and stared at the dead outlaw, for whom he had a great deal of respect. Then he did a strange thing: he propped Doolin's body up in the bed and fired a blast of buckshot into his chest.

The distraught widow condemned the lawman bitterly for defiling her husband's body in death, but she soon learned the reason for his seemingly brutal act. Thomas claimed that he had killed Doolin in battle, thereby collecting the reward money for his capture. It was a king's ransom—but Thomas never kept a penny of it. He gave every cent to Bill Doolin's widow!